James K. Hosmer

The Color-Guard

being a corporal's notes of military service in the Nineteenth Army Corps

James K. Hosmer

The Color-Guard
being a corporal's notes of military service in the Nineteenth Army Corps

ISBN/EAN: 9783337886059

Printed in Europe, USA, Canada, Australia, Japan

Cover: Foto ©Andreas Hilbeck / pixelio.de

More available books at **www.hansebooks.com**

THE

COLOR-GUARD:

BEING

A CORPORAL'S NOTES OF MILITARY SERVICE
IN THE NINETEENTH ARMY CORPS.

BY

JAMES K. HOSMER,

OF THE FIFTY-SECOND REGIMENT MASS. VOLUNTEERS.

" Till we called
Both field and city ours, we never stood
To ease our breasts with panting."
CORIOLANUS, Act II. Scene 2.

BOSTON:

WALKER, WISE, AND COMPANY,

245, WASHINGTON STREET.

1864.

BOSTON:
STEREOTYPED AND PRINTED BY JOHN WILSON AND SON,
No. 5 Water Street.

TO

HALBERT STEVENS GREENLEAF,

LATE COLONEL OF THE FIFTY-SECOND REGIMENT MASS. VOLUNTEERS,

A Resolute Soldier and Noble Man,

𝕿𝖍𝖎𝖘 𝕭𝖔𝖔𝖐 𝖎𝖘 𝖗𝖊𝖘𝖕𝖊𝖈𝖙𝖋𝖚𝖑𝖑𝖞 𝕴𝖓𝖘𝖈𝖗𝖎𝖇𝖊𝖉

BY

ONE WHO HAS WITNESSED HIS COURAGE, AND EXPERIENCED
HIS GOODNESS.

INTRODUCTION.

As this volume sees the light at the instance of the author's friends, and with much diffidence and reluctance on his part, it may not be inappropriate for one of those friends to give a brief statement of the history of the work, and of the reasons why its publication has seemed desirable.

In September, 1862, Rev. JAMES K. HOSMER, pastor of the First Church in Deerfield, Mass., having but recently entered on his chosen profession with ardor and with rich promise of success, heard, in the needs of his country, a higher call of duty; and with every motive of interest and personal feeling opposed to the measure, but with a sense of obligation which his conscience would not set aside, he enlisted as a private in the Fifty-second Regiment of Massachusetts Volunteers. He entered the service with the determination to evade neither labor, hardship, nor peril; to devote whatever there was in him of capacity and vigor to the public cause; and to do what he might, not as a clergyman, but as a Christian man, to minister to the physical and moral welfare of his fellow-soldiers. His ability and culture early procured for him the offer of a safe and easy post in the military family of Gen. Banks. This he declined; accepting no preferment, save a place, in the fore-front of peril, as one of the corporals intrusted with the defence of the colors of his regiment. During his term of service, he prepared letters, in the form of a journal, with no thought of their publication, but solely for the perusal of his father's family and of certain intimate friends, to whom they were sent in turn. They were read with vivid interest; and there gradually grew, among several of those through whose hands they passed, a strong desire that the pleasure and benefit derived from them should be extended to a larger circle. It is in deference to their judgment that he consented to revise the journal, and to commit it to the press.

We have urged the publication of this record on the following grounds :—It is the narrative of one who gave every possible proof of disinterested patriotism. The writer had large and varied opportunities of observation; and with them he possessed keen, quick, and accurate discernment, and, as we think, a superior power of life-like description and narration. His journal gives a faithful picture of the privations, sufferings, and perils of those whose living and dying sacrifice is the costly price at which we are purchasing the redemption of our country from dismemberment and ruin; and it can hardly fail to do its part in awakening the gratitude we owe to those who have gone forth in the defence of our liberties and institutions. It commends our army to our warmest sympathy. and to those offices of relief and comfort by which we may lighten the burdens of our soldiers, and solace ·those who return from the camp or the battle-field maimed, crippled, and invalids. It is also the journal of one who carried with him to the service tender and humane fellow-feeling for his companions in peril; and we prize it for the unostentatious benevolence and kindness which it breathes, and which made the author's life as a soldier parallel and congenial with the quiet scenes of pastoral duty from which only the imperative demands of a holy cause could have led him to turn aside. While the work, on these grounds, proffers high claims on the public regard, it is believed that its literary execution is worthy of the reputation which the author has already attained, and will hereafter realize, in the sacred calling to which he has consecrated his powers and his life.

Less than this we could not say; more than this we need not; so much as this the author's modesty would not suffer, were this Introduction to meet his eye before it becomes indelibly a part of his book.

A. P. PEABODY.

CAMBRIDGE, Oct. 22, 1863.

CONTENTS.

IV.

THE DAY OF CLOUDS AND THICK DARKNESS.

V.

SUSPENSE.

VI.

"INTO THE LION'S MOUTH."

VII.

FALLING BACK.

VIII.

THE GARDEN OF LOUISIANA.

IX.

VICTORY.

X.

PURSUIT.

XI.

ON THE BAYOU COURTABLEAU.

XII.

IN THE HOSPITAL.

XIII.

BATTLE.

XIV.

THE WOLF AT BAY.

XV.

TRIUMPH.

XVI.

CONCLUSION.

THE COLOR-GUARD.

INTRODUCTION.

Camp Miller, Greenfield, Mass., Nov. 13, 1862.

Dear P——, — To-night there are in the tent at least fifteen men. There are three sets of men playing cards. I sit at one end of our table, close under the shelving edge of the tent, with head bent over to get rid of the slant of the canvas. My seat is a heap of straw, covered with a blanket. A kerosene lamp gives light to me on one side, and to a set at whist on the other. It is cold out of doors; but the tent is in a sweat, with its stove, and crowd of men. Slap go the cards on to the table. Every moment comes up some point for debate. Throughout the tent there is loud and constant talking, sometimes swearing; generally good-natured, sometimes ill-natured.

You want to know why I have left my pulpit and parish, and enlisted. I had several reasons; all plain, simple, and sensible enough. I have believed in the war from the first. The cause of the North, briefly, is, to me, the cause of civilization and liberty To help this, I have preached, made speeches, and talked in private. Ought I not to practise what I preach?

1*   [9]

Ought I to shrink from encountering perils and hardships which I have urged others to encounter?

Then, again, having no family, I can go better than many others in our village, — men liable to be draughted, whose means are straitened, and who have wives and children to support. These are my main reasons; but, besides these, I confess to a love for adventure. Moreover, I hope to gain new robustness from the exposure. I own, also, to something of a military spirit. In every honorable war since the settlement of the country, I believe, some member of the stock from which I am descended has taken part. Generally, these ancestors of mine have been in very humble positions; although my great-grandfather held an important command among the militia at Concord Bridge, and did much toward keeping the "embattled farmers" firm on that day before the British volleys. In our family traditions he is an illustrious character, together with his brother, "Uncle Ben," a sturdy husbandman, who fought faithfully that day throughout the long pursuit, and afterward carried a heavy old blunderbuss in many a hard campaign. I own, it is a sort of fame I covet, — to have my name go down in our modest family annals as the parson, who, in his generation, went with rifle on shoulder to Texas or Louisiana or the Carolinas; doing his duty in honorable fields, as did great-grandfather and "Uncle Ben" of old.

I trust that the motives I have put first were the ones that influenced me for the most part; but these last, too, have had their weight.

Ed., my young brother, you know, has been made first sergeant of the company. He goes round, therefore, with a broad stripe down each leg, and a blue diamond, with a triple underscoring, upon each arm, — insignia upon which we poor privates and corporals look with reverence. I am now one of the eight corporals whose duty it is to guard the colors. I have a narrow stripe running down each pantaloon, and a double bar, or chevron, on each arm. Ed. and I button up to the chin in our blue and brass; and are a brilliant pair, I assure you.

There seems to be no doubt now about our going with Gen. Banks. We hope it will be soon; for, although we are decently comfortable here, we should prefer some sweet-potato patch for a camp-ground, to this pumpkin-field.

Yours very truly,

THE "CORPORAL."

CHAPTER I.

THE THRESHOLD.

Nov 23, 1862. — I propose to keep a diary of my soldiering, and am now making my first entry. Brother Ed. and I are going to the war together. He is nineteen, and leaves a clerk's desk in an insurance-office. I am older, and leave a minister's study. It is the 52d Regiment of Massachusetts Volunteers. I am in our little tent at Camp N P Banks, not far from Jamaica, in Long Island. The tent is perhaps eight feet square, and meant for seven soldiers. A leg of ham partly devoured, with gnawed loaves of bread and some tin cups, lies just at my right foot. Corporal Buffum, six feet and two or three inches tall, is writing home, just at the other foot. Joseph McGill is sleeping, wrapped up in his rubber blanket. The floor of the tent, at the sides, is covered with knapsacks, blankets, and soldiers' furniture. Silloway, a black-whiskered, fine-looking soldier, puts his head in, but, to my relief, does not enter; for where could I put him while I write?

We left Camp Miller, where the Fifty-second organized, two or three days ago. For the first time, the knapsacks, full-loaded, were packed on, the canteens were filled, the haversacks were crammed with two days' rations. It was a heavy load as we set off in a cold November rain, nearly a thousand of us, bending over, and with pants rolled up. It rained harder and harder: but Greenfield streets were filled with people; and the nearer we came to the depot, the thicker the crowd. Then came the last parting and hand-shaking: eyes were full, and lips on a tremble. The heart came out grandly in some of the fellows.

At midnight we reached New Haven. Ed. had been on guard at the car-door in the drizzle, and now came off duty. We trundled on to the steamboat-wharf, climbed out, and formed in two lines; many of the boys turning round for their first sight and sniff at salt-water. The "Traveller" was at hand, aboard which, rank after rank, we marched, — on top, between decks, into cabin below, and saloon above.

The morning was gray and wet. It poured as we stood on the forward deck; but my rubber blanket shed the rain, and my havelock, of the same material, kept it off head and neck. On upper deck and lower deck, and through every window, one could see the crowding hundreds, — curious faces, bearded and smooth; dripping blankets and caps; the white string of the canteen crossing the band of the haversack upon the breast. Stout fellows they were, almost all; the pick, for spirit and strength, of two counties. You would not think men were scarce; but I remembered the poor old village, and its Shakspeare Club of fifteen young girls, and only one young fellow available as a beau.

Past great ships, past iron-clads fitting out at the Novelty Works, past the Navy Yard, now down between the two great cities and around the Battery, and stop at a North-river pier, — haversack on one shoulder, canteen on the other. "Now, Silas Dibble, hook on my knapsack, and I will hook on yours;" rubber blanket over all; then helmet, with the long flap down on the shoulders. The march begins. Dirty and hungry we go through the muddy streets. I tread, almost, in old tracks of mine; no longer in broadcloth and patent leathers, but with the iron heel of war well greased with neat's-foot. Halt in the Park.

The boot-blacking business is stagnant. The "Astor" is gray, hard, and inhospitable like the heavens. "Times," "Tribune," and "World" look at us through all their windows, as if they were hungry for an item. It pours and pours. We wind in a long string across the Park; then, in a long string, back again; then, at the end of all the purposeless winding, we come to a purposeless halt.

Ankle-deep, at last, through the mud into the Park Barracks, to breakfast on coarse but wholesome soup. Did any thing ever relish so? Then they take pity on us, and let us go into the City Hall, whose stone corridors we swarm through; and before long the regiment, in good part, is asleep. I go off with my back against a marble pillar. By and by we must fall in again. Ed. is irreverently screaming, "Fall in, Company D!" at the top of his voice, through that echoing marble centre of metropolitan splendor and dignity. The regiment marches up Broadway, is cheered, and, I believe, praised; and climbs, at last, into the great barracks in Franklin Street.

Next day we have a march before us of eight or nine miles, — through Broadway and Grand Street, over the Ferry, into the suburbs; through filth and splendor, mud in the street, brown stone and marble at the side. The drums at the head of the column hardly sound midway down the regiment, through the roar; but we keep our step, and dress across in a tolerable line. Past factories, where sooty faces crowd to the doors; past sugar-refineries, where men, stripped to the waist, come to the windows; past Dutch groceries by the hundred; into a district of cabbage-gardens at last; then into a chaos of brick-kilns, rope-walks, and desolate grave-yards.

We tramp in over the old Union race-track at length, upon the enclosed grassy space, and are at our camp-ground. Dreary, dismal, miserable. No overcoats; all perspiration with our march under the burden; no chance for tea or coffee, or any thing warm: a sorry prospect, boys, for comfort to-night. But never mind. Behold how the Yankee will vindicate himself in the face of the worst fortune! Fences are stripped of rails; and we have blazing fires in no time, which make the inhospitable, leaden sky speedily blush for itself. Rubber blankets are tacked together, and tents extemporized. Corporal Buffum, Ed., and I, strike a solemn league. We find two sticks and a long rail. We drive the sticks into the ground for uprights, then lay the rail on top.

Buffum and I tack our blankets together with strings through the eyelet-holes. We place the joining along the cross-timber, letting the blankets slope away, roof-fashion, on each side toward the ground, fastening them at the edges with pegs, and strings straining them tight. Then we spread Ed.'s rubber on the ground underneath, put our luggage at one end, and crowd in to try the effect. We have to pack in tight, big Buffum and Ed. not leaving much room for me; but the closer the better. The north-wind blows, and the air threatens snow. We survey our wigwam with great admiration. I lie down for the night with revolver and dirk strapped one on each side, unwashed, bedraggled, and armed like Jack Sheppard himself. We freeze along through the hours. We get into one another's arms to keep warm as we can, and shiver through till daylight.

When morning comes, all is confusion. The regiment looks as if it had rained down. It is clear, but raw. No chance to wash now, nor all day long. Our tents come. We pitch them in long rows, well ordered; floor them from fences near by; and carpet them with straw and marsh hay. Six or seven of us pack in here like sardines in a box, lying on our sides, "spoon-fashion."

Nov. 26. — To-day is wretched enough. All night long, whenever I woke up, it was pitter-patter on the canvas; and this morning it is a drizzle, which turns the clay outside into puttyish mud, — mud which plays Damon; my boot-soles appearing in the *rôle* of Pythias, — I earnestly hope, for this occasion only; for the friendship is too fervent. No fire, or prospect of any; for the load of hard wood which was pitched off in front of the tents yesterday is too wet to be kindled. We have heaped the straw up to the sides of the tent, and covered it with blankets. It makes a good seat for us; and four or five of us are writing here, our feet in the central space. The whole thing is only a little larger than an old-fashioned four-post bedstead. Our feet are dove-tailed in among one another; the boots all buff, clear above the ankles, with sloppy clay.

Our guns were issued to us the other day, beautiful pieces, of the most improved pattern, — the Springfield rifled musket of 1862. Mine is behind me now, dark black-walnut stock, well oiled, so that the beauty of the wood is brought out, hollowed at the base, and smoothly fitted with steel, to correspond exactly to the curve of the shoulder, against which I shall have to press it many and many a time. The spring of the lock, just stiff and just limber enough; the eagle and stamp of the Government pressed into the steel plate; barrel, long and glistening, — bound into its bed by gleaming rings, — long and straight, and so bright, that when I present arms, and bring it before my face, I can see nose and spectacles and the heavy beard on lip and chin, which already the camp is beginning to develop. Then the bayonet, straight and tapering, dazzling under a sun-ray, grooved delicately, — as if it were meant to illustrate problems in conic sections, — smooth to the finger as a surface of glass, and coming to a point sharp as a needle.

We have dress-parades now; and, the other afternoon, I was a spectator instead of taking part. The Fifty-second is formed four deep. I have often seen them in line at Camp Miller; but now we have our arms, and look more like soldiers. Four deep, and how long the line is! They are still as men can be at the parade rest. Now, from the right flank, come marching the drums down the line; slow time; every eye to the front; the colonel, hand upon sword-hilt, facing them all, — tall, straight, soldierly, his silver eagles on each shoulder. The drums have reached the end of the line, and turn. First a long, brisk roll, thrice repeated; then back along the line with quicker time and step, round the right flank again, past the adjutant; the thrice-repeated roll again sounding muffled, as it comes to me through the now intervening line of men, — a peculiar throb, as if it were inside of the head. It is the adjutant's turn. He is at his place in front of the line. "First sergeants to the front and centre!" Ten soldiers, strait, sash at waist, march forward, and, one by one, report. It is Ed.'s turn now, tall, fine, bright-eyed soldier that he is. His gloved hand gives the salute; and I hear him, through the music of other regiments, "Fourth company all present or accounted for." Buttoned up to the chin he is, in his dress-coat; his sash, with bright revolver belt, outside; his gun at his shoulder with true martial poise. "First sergeants to your posts!" It is the turn of the commissioned officers. They step out to the front, in full-dress uniform, a fine-looking row of men; then march forward, with brave, unanimous step, in a brilliant, glittering line. It is over, and visitors near step up to me to inquire about the regiment. I feel proud of the men, proud of the colonel, proud of the brilliant officers who have marched forward to salute in concert, — the white-gloved hands simultaneously at the visor. Back go the companies into the streets of the camp, under the first sergeants. I am proud to see how Ed. gets his company by the flank, and promptly manœuvres them.

We have had a flag presented to us; but it is too splendid and heavy for actual service. Our real flag, for service, is more modest, and yet handsome; of silk, floating from a staff of ash; the name of the regiment printed in gold upon one of the crimson stripes. As the wind comes off the bay to us at battalion-drill, the heavy silk brushes my cheek. We shall know each other well during these coming months. I take off my bayonet, and invert it, that it may not wound the flag it is to defend. So does jovial Bias Dickinson, the corporal who is my file leader, and the rest of the guard. We have also the white flag of Massachusetts, the Indian and uplifted sword upon a snowy field; plain enough, when the breeze smooths it out, for the senior captain to see from his post on the right flank, and Sergt. Jones, right general guide, whose post is still farther off. When drill is over, we must guard our charge to the colonel's tent, roll the crimson and azure folds carefully about the staff, and put them under shelter; then our day's work is done.

CHAPTER II.

THE TRANSPORT.

Nov. 29. — This is the steamer " Illinois," in the stream, about half a mile off the Battery. The ship is preparing to sail. Evening ; and by special courtesy, the surgeon being absent, I am invited to sleep in his berth to-night. No slight favor, you folks whose sheets are clean, to have a mattress softer than an oaken-deck plank ; and a place to lay one's head, sweeter than a bundle of old rope, soiled by the muddy feet of a trampling army. I stand up, portfolio in hand, half sitting, half leaning, against the cabin-table, with back toward the dim light. A throng of officers are writing, talking, and hurrying past. Now I am luckier : I have found a stool under a brighter light, and the cleanest and best place I have had to write my journal in since I began it.

Yesterday we marched to Brooklyn ; then went off through lanterned vessels at dusk, past the glowing city, until at last the " Illinois " threw over us the shadow of her black hull and double stacks. We waited an hour in the cold, on the lighter ; then another on the open deck, among the gun-carriages of a battery that was going with us. We were suffered at last to crowd into the cabin, all grumblers. Ed. could hardly make himself heard, though his lungs are good.

The wrath of the regiment vented itself in every form, — the oath, the deprecation, the remonstrance. Tom Barker fairly *blued* the air about him with vocal brimstone and sulphur, — a most accomplished and full-lunged blasphemer. From him, there was every gradation down to a little fellow who remonstrated with a gentle spill of milk and water.

Camp down, soldiers, where you can! This cabin is stripped of furniture and carpet: a mirror and the white paint are the only things to remind one of the old elegance of the packet. I glance at the glass as we crowd in. Which am I among the bearded, blue-coated, hustling men? I hardly know myself, sunburnt and muddied; the "52," on the cap top, showing out in the lantern light. Sergt. Warriner, of Company A, — gentlemanly fellow, — left guide, whose elbow rubs mine at battalion-drill, offers me a place in a "bunk" he has found empty in one of the staterooms. Bias Dickinson, my wise and jovial file-leader, bunks over me. There is room for another: so I go out to where McGill is wedged into the crowding mass, and extract him as I would a tooth. Gradually the hubbub is quelled. The mass of men, like a river seeking its level, flows into "bunk" and stateroom, cabin and galley. Then the floors are covered, and a few miserable ones hold on to banisters and table-legs, and at last the regiment swears itself into an uncomfortable sleep.

Nov. 30. —We woke up the morning after we came aboard, — Warriner, Bias, and I. Company D woke up generally on the cabin-floor. Poor Companies H and F woke up down in the hold. What to do for breakfast? Through the hatchway opposite our state-room-door, we could see the waiters in the lower cabin setting tables for the commissioned officers. Presently there was a steam of coffee and steaks; then a long row of shoulder-straps, and a clatter of knives and forks; we, meanwhile, breakfastless, and undergoing the torments of Tantalus.

But we cannot make out a very strong case of hardship. Beef, hard-bread, and coffee were soon ready. Bill Hilson, in a marvellous cap of pink and blue, cut up the big joints on a gun-box. The "non-coms," whose chevrons take them past the guard amidships, went out loaded with the tin cups of the men to Hen. Hilson, — out through cabin-door, through greasy, crowded passage-way, behind the wheel, to the galley, where, over a mammoth, steaming caldron, Hen., through the vapor, pours out coffee by the pailful. Hen. looks like a beneficent genius, — one of the "Arabian Nights" sort, —just being condensed from the smoke and mist of these blessed hot kettles. He drips, and almost simmers, with perspiration, as if he had hardly gone half-way yet from vapor to flesh.

I have been down the brass-plated staircase, into the splendors of the commissioned-officers' cabin, — really nothing great at all; but luxurious as compared with our quarters, already greasy from rations, and stained with tobacco-juice; and sumptuous beyond words, as compared with the unplaned boards and tarry odors of the quarters of the privates. Have I mentioned that now our places are assigned? The "non-coms"— non-commissioned, meaning, not *non compos;* though evil-minded high privates declare it might well mean that — have assigned to them an upper cabin, with staterooms, over the quarters of the officers, in the after-part of the ship. The privates are in front, on the lower decks, and in the hold. I promise, in a day or two, to play Virgil, and conduct you through the dismal circles of this Malebolge. Now I speak of the cabin of the officers. The hatches are open above and below, to the upper deck and into the hold. Down the hatch goes a dirty stream of commissary-stores, gun-carriages, rifled-cannon, and pressed hay, within an inch or two of cut-glass, gilt-mouldings, and mahogany. The third mate, with voice coarse and deep as the grating of ten-ton packages along the skids, orders this and that, or bays inarticulately in a growl at a shirking sailor.

Five sergeants of our company, and two corporals of us, have a stateroom together, — perhaps six feet by eight. Besides us, two officers' servants consider that they have a right here. Did any one say, "Elbow-room"?

Dec. 1. — Each man now has his place for the voyage assigned him: so, if you can climb well, let us go down, and see the men below. It is right through the damp, crowded passage at the side of the paddle-wheel first. Here is a fence and a gate, impervious to the private; but in his badge the corporal possesses the potent golden bough which gains him ingress through here into Hades. Just amidships, we go in through a door from the upper deck. This first large space is the hospital; already with thirty or forty in its rough, unplaned bunks. From this, what is half-stairway and half-ladder leads down the hatch. A lantern is burning here; and we see that the whole space between decks, not very great, is filled with bunks, — three rows of them between floor and ceiling, — stretching away into darkness on every hand, with two-feet passages winding among them. "Hullo!" from a familiar voice. I look up and down, and off into the darkness. "Hullo!" again. It is from overhead. Sile Dibble, sure.

Here is another corner, behind a post, where is the pock-marked face of little Hines. (The business of Hines has been that of a "gigger:" puzzle over that, as I did.) I hear the salutes of men, but cannot see their faces; for it is beyond the utmost efforts of the little lantern to show them up. Presently I go on through the narrow passage, with populous bunks, humming with men, on each side, — three layers between deck and deck. I can only hear them, and once in a while dimly see a face. At length we come to a railing, over which we climb, and descend another ladder, into regions still darker, — submarine, I believe, or, at any rate, on a level with the sea. Here swings another lantern. Up overhead, through deck after deck, is a skylight, which admits light, and wet too, from above.

It is like looking from the bottom of a well; and pretty uncomfortable is the truth that lies at the bottom of this well.

As above, so here again, there are three tiers of bunks, with the narrow passages among them. The men lie side by side, with but two feet or so of space; but are in good spirits, though sepulchred after this fashion. I should know this gray, knit cap, with its blue button, — McGill, in the top row, his toes within easy reach of the beams above; and Silloway comes crawling over, from regions more remote, to shake hands. Gottlieb, our small German, is in the centre tier; and in the lower row, just above the bolts of the deck, is Gunn, the old campaigner. The air seems not bad. It is dark in the day-time, except right under the skylight. A fortnight or so from now, a poor, emaciated crowd, I fear, it will be proceeding from these lower deeps of the "Illinois." I go back with an uneasy conscience to our six feet by eight up above, so infinitely preferable to these quarters of the privates, though five big sergeants with their luggage share it with me, and two waiters have no other home; so that we overflow through door and window, on to the deck and floor outside.

Ed. and I turn in at half-past eight, lying on our sides, and interrupting one another's sleep with, "Look out for your elbow!" "I am going over the edge!" "You will press me through into the Company C bunks!" This morning I took breakfast in the berth, — dining-room, study, and parlor, as well. There is

2

room enough, sitting Turk-fashion, and bending over. Sergt. Hannum carves the lump of boiled beef with my dirk. "Jest the thing, I van!" December spits at us with miserable rain, like a secession lady. The steam of the officers' soup comes up; but the gong does not mean us.

Dec. 2. — "Sail to-day!" That has been the morning song aboard the "Illinois" ever since the Fifty-second piled itself into its darknesses. It was so Saturday, Sunday, and Monday. We came to believe it did not mean any thing: so, Tuesday morning being fair, Buffum and I got permission to go ashore, smiling at the superb joke of the officer when he warned us to be "back in a couple of hours, for we surely sail to-day." But, when we came aboard again, the anchor was really up; and the "Illinois," no longer twirled by the tide about its thumbs, began to show a will of its own, and was soon moving seaward with its deeply burdened bosom and swarming decks. Our orders were sealed, and the colonel could not open them until twenty-four hours after sailing. We could not know, then, until the morrow, whither the wheels, the tide, and the strong stern-wind, were bearing us; but the prow was southward, and the Fifty-second was content. Distance washes the spire of "Trinity" out of the northern sky; the Narrows, grim with forts and prisons, now grow narrower; and soon Sandy Hook, the beckoning finger which the old Navesink hills fling out for ever to invite inbound ships, lets us slide past its curving knuckle fairly out to sea. All goes well, with no motion but

the throb of the engine. They light the lanterns on
the wheel-house and in the fore-top; they light them
between-decks, swinging gently while a soldier reads
his Testament, or a party play cards.

I fear we are reduced to the condition of not having
a single unprincipled fellow in our present mess of non-
coms, — a very dire calamity to a party of campaigners.
Rogers is a man of character and dignity, — an
ex town-official; round-faced Sergt. Brown is far too
exemplary to grumble much, or hook dainty morsels of
prog for himself and his "pals;" Hannum never
swears, but only "vans" and "vums;" while Grosvenor, the teacher, has walked in virtue so long before
his pupils, he is much too far gone ever to be developed
into your proper, easy-conscienced "soger-boy." When
beef is scarce, who shall bribe the cabin-waiters, or
steal tidbits from the galley? Can we survive it, when
the coffee fails, not to have one at least to be mouthpiece
to the collective wrath of the company, through whom
we may vicariously pour our choler upon the commissary?

Dec. 3. — I resolve I will try a night with the men
in the hold. Elnathan Gunn, the old soldier, invites
me to share his bed and board. Life on a transport
becomes so simplified, that bed and board become one;
the soldier softening his plank with his haversack of
beef and biscuit for a mattress and pillow.

'Tis half-past eight at night as I climb down in night-
rig, — blowze and knit cap, with round button at the
top, like Charles Lamb's "great Panjandrum himself."

It is comfortable; but Ed.'s fraternal partiality turns to disgust whenever I put it on. I stoop low, — it is the lowest tier of bunks, — climb over two prostrate men, then lie down sandwiched helplessly between two slices of timber above and below, where I go to sleep among the raw-head and bloody-bone stories of Elnathan Gunn. I wake up at midnight hot and stifled, as if I were in a mine caved in. "Gunn, give me my boots!" Gunn fishes them out of some hole in the dark. I tug at the straps, half stifled, bump my head as I rise, grovel on my stomach out over two or three snorers, and hurry through the dark for the upper deck, thankful that, being corporal, I can have quarters where I can see and breathe. Through the cabin, over slumbering drums and drummers, — for the music, too, is privileged to remain above, — then in by the side of Ed. We heard, at noon, we were bound for Ship Island; and, while I am hoping for plenty of air and good weather the rest of the voyage, down shut the eyelids, and consciousness is guillotined for the night.

Dec. 8. — I have had no heart or ability to make an entry in my journal for days and days; but, this morning, sea-sickness is gone, the sea is smooth, the weather is July for sun, with a soft, September wind breathing just astern. It is entirely comfortable for me to sit in my shirt-sleeves on the hurricane-deck. How sweet is this calm and soft air! The white lighthouse, at the southern point of Cape Florida, stands three or four miles to the west of us. We slide on rapidly over coral-reefs; the water blue as opal; a sail here and there on the horizon; and in the distance, like round, green bosses, the thickly scattered Keys of Florida, — studs of chrysoprase, with which this sumptuous southern sea fastens the opal covering down over its pearl-lit caves and coral groves. It is something rare, this coloring of the sea. I have just raised my eyes to look westward. Close at hand, the water is blue, with the ordinary deep-sea tinge; but just beyond, over a bar of snowy sand it must be, it is green as malachite, wonderfully clear and living.

Sunday morning, Brown, who rises early, came back to us with the news of a death in the regiment during the night. The soldier's body lay upon the hurricane-deck, sewed up in his blanket, ready for its burial in the sea. We do not reach Ship Island until Wednesday or Thursday of this week, and shall make no port before.

It is noon when the funeral takes place. I am lying in my berth, still weak, when I hear the voice of the chaplain, on the deck just over me, beginning the funeral service. I hurry up. They swing the American flag at half-mast just over the body, and as many of the regiment as it is safe to admit to that part of the ship stand around. The service is very impressive. A choir of soldiers sing a hymn; then a kinsman of the dead man lifts the plank; down it descends, weighted at the feet. Tropical fish play about the ship. The northern breeze, right from home, breathes over the ocean-grave; the clear-green sea closes above, — a sepulchre of emerald, — a sad and sudden end for the poor Shelburne boy.

The keel of the ship grates upon the bottom. The captain jumps to the wheel, and it is about immediately, until land fades again, and it is once more "one wide water all around us." The sun sets gloriously behind this land of romance. A soft crimson haze hangs over the land, and smokes up zenithward like rich fume and vapor from old Ponce de Leon's fountain of youth. A splendor of cloud and light is thrown upon the west, — tall buttressed pillars glowing in the light, as if the powers of the air had begun to paint there the proud escutcheon of the Spanish kings. In another moment, I shall behold the crowned shield and the rampant lions; but it fades, and now to the eastward rises the moon. The sky to-night is vapory, with fine, clear lines of azure running through the vapor, like veins, — veins how blue and deep! as if filled with the blue blood of the true Hidalgos of old Castile.

There has been no end to grumbling. We have all been sea-sick, and responsibilities which the disordered stomach ought to shoulder have been thrown on the food. This brings me to speak of what I have noticed again and again since we became soldiers, — that the first to complain are those who have come from the poorest circumstances. Those who at home have been forced to live on the coarsest food are now first and loudest in their outcries against the rations.

Before we left New York, McGill and I clubbed together to buy Prof. Cairnes's book, — "The Slave Power;" a purchase I am glad enough we made. I have read the book attentively during the voyage, with great interest, and feel now doubly strong to fight for the Union cause. I respect England and her writers. I have been accustomed to defer very much to English thinkers; and though, in the exercise of my most con-· scientious judgment, I could not help thinking our cause was right, yet I have not been able to feel quite easy and satisfied when the voices of intelligent Englishmen seemed so generally against us. It was very cheering when the "National" came, a few months ago, with a fine article on our side; then the "Westminster," with Mill's strong presentation of our case. Now here is this new book, by a writer, to be sure, who seems to be only just rising into note, but evidently a man of very fine powers, and sure to wield a profound influence. How his analysis of the matter carries conviction with it! How plain it is that the hopes of civilization depend upon the triumph of the North! There is a grand sentence, which Cairnes quotes from De Tocqueville, to the effect, "that when a people are striving for independence, whether the effort has right or wrong on its side, depends upon *what they want independence for*, — whether to govern themselves, or to tyrannize over others." "Down with slavery!" though I own my sympathies go as much or more with the suffering whites than the suffering blacks. I believe good has come, and is coming, to the black serf through his contact with the Anglo-Saxon, though it has been so rough and harsh; and probably the suffering of the race, great as it is, is not much greater than it would have been if they had remained in unenslaved barbarism.

But how terrible is the corruption which slavery brings upon the master class! Thanks to this good book! Now Dixie — Ship Island — is full in sight; and I can put my foot confidently upon its sand if we come to land, buttressed in my feelings that I have right on my side, though I come armed against its owners.

Dec. 14. — We are in one of the passes of the Mississippi, on our way to New Orleans. It is Sunday again, — our third aboard the ship, — and a most lovely day to be introduced to Louisiana. It is a perfect summer day, with the bulging clouds and blue sky of a hay-day at home, though there is breeze enough to keep it from being oppressively hot. We only hope the "rebs" are as much in the dark as to our destination as the expedition itself and the people of the North generally.

We left Ship Island yesterday, — Saturday; having lain at anchor there since Thursday. Sergt. Hannum went ashore there, and came back smacking his lips, and telling great stories of a hoe-cake, with butter, which he bought of a contraband. He must have had a good supper, and became the pet and star of the non-coms for that evening, who made him repeat his story again and again, endeavoring, from the lusciousness of his descriptions, to realize the actual sensations which the palate of the lucky sergeant had experienced.

On Saturday morning, in came huge steamer after steamer; among them the "North Star," the flag-ship, with Gen. Banks. Boats, with staff-officers, sped from vessel to vessel, — one to ours; and news presently came from the cabin, we were to sail again as soon as steam could be raised.

All day long, transports, laden with troops, were arriving, — the swift " Matanzas ; " the immense " Arago ; " at length the familiar " Atlantic," in which I once took a voyage ; she and her consort the " Baltic," with others, large and small. The decks of all are dark with troops. We hear from some the drum and fife ; from others the strains of a full band ; and, from every regiment, cheer after cheer as they round the point of the island, pass in among the ships, and finally cast anchor. A gunboat comes up ; lies-to off the point ; and presently up at the fore goes a string of flags, one over the other, — at the top, a red and white checker ; then a blue, bisected by a white line ; then a red and white, the line of division between the two colors running diagonally from corner to corner. I turn my head toward the men-of-war lying in the harbor, and see that they, too, have strings of flags flying. They are talking with those gay, fluttering tongues across the intervening mile or two. What do they say? Presently the slate-colored hull, with the black guns looking from its sides, is cutting the water again, and she casts anchor among the fleet.

There is no lack of excitement to-day. By noon, there must be some twelve thousand troops at the anchorage, on steamers large and small.

The " North Star," with the general, weighs anchor again, the blue flag of pre-eminence flying at the fore ; then the " Spaulding ; " then another and another ;

2*

until, at length, our turn comes. Round go the wheels again : we pass the point, and are at sea, the "Arago" following in our wake, and others, whose smoke only we can see, far in the rear of her.

Night falls. There are moving lights ahead, behind, and at each side, where the ships are finding their way. Word comes up from the cabin that we are bound for New Orleans, but not to stop ; and we remain as much in the dark as ever about our final goal. It only leaks out that the colonel has said, " No one yet has named our true destination." Ed. and I sit on deck, as night after night we have done. Arthur Sprague, Lieut. Haskell, and one or two others, pour out far over the sea some Saturday-night hymns, in which I am glad to join. There I sit, and into my mind come thoughts of the world's great expeditions, — of Mardonius in a purple, Persian galley, with the other satraps and their master Xerxes sweeping down to where Themistocles and the line of Athenian triremes waited for them at Salamis ; then of the great Duke of Medina Sidonia leading his armada towards St. George's Channel, while the Prince of Parma, on the Netherland coast, impatiently watched for the signal for launching forth with his brave Spanish infantry. Did the old Medean spearmen sit, I wonder, with dangling legs, looking as unromantic as Corporal Hardiker there, with his greasy pantaloons half up to his knee ? or did bearded, old musketeers, in casques and burgonets, sing songs of Aragon and Leon, as we sing the songs of Yankee-land ? My thoughts are not auspicious, I fancy ;

for almost every expedition that comes to mind, as I sit, goes out in a bad cause, and ends in disaster. I would not yield my cause for any that man ever upheld, though so many would class us with Persia and Spain in injustice. How full of romance are these seas, with their great associations, — Balboa and De Soto, galleons with glittering adventurers, buccaneers, mariners of Genoa and Portugal in gilded argosies!

Ed. and I go below, to wake up toward daylight, and find the engines still, and hear the hoarse shout of the gruff third mate, " Watch ! " as he heaves the lead. We are just off the Bar, at the mouth of one of the passes ; and, when we come on deck, the pilot-schooner is flying from one to another among the fleet of steamers, — who, like us, are all lying-to, — putting her pilots here and there. We take on ours. In a moment the heaving sea is behind us, its blue a thing of the past ; and we breast the sallow current of the Mississippi, with coarse, strange-looking sedges, ten feet high, on the banks ; fish-huts here and there ; spoonbills flying about in flocks ; and, as I live, a pelican, — symbolic bird, — pocketing fish out of the river. The bank gradually begins to look more firm ; though often the sea stretches away close at hand beyond the narrow ridge of earth, which is the only shore. Toward noon, we reach the famous forts, whose walls are low, but covered with formidable guns, one of which gives us a salute as we come up.

In the course of the afternoon, we pass a plantation, belonging, so the pilot says, to Judah P. Benjamin.

It is one of the finest we see during the sail, with large sugar-houses, comfortable cabins, and a stately mansion. We go within a stone's-throw of the groves and balconies, sweet with aromas and soft breezes as the haunts of Circe, — the nursery-spots of hideous treason. A crowd of negroes, of all sizes and both sexes, rush to the bank to shout, and wave their hands. The only expressions of joy we witness are from the blacks: indeed, they are almost the sole population remaining here. The mules in the cane-fields are driven by black drivers, and blacks are the only figures we see about the sugar-mills. The streets of negro cabins are often populous; but the master's mansion, almost invariably, stands with no sign of life within its grove.

We go below for supper. When we return to the deck, night has fallen; and, in front, we can just begin to see the lights of New Orleans. To the right of the city, in the heavens, glares a conflagration, red, like a great light we saw the night of our arrival at Ship Island, said then to be toward Mobile, and perhaps the signal-fire of the enemy. Ed. and I sit on the paddle-box, watching the light, — the hostile city, in chains and under our cannon. Now we are close upon it. At our side lies the "North Star;" when plunge goes the anchor, with its rattling chain, in twenty-five fathoms water. All is mystery about us, except that, through the night, the invisible city looks at us through its blinking lights, — eyes alone visible, like the wolf that Putnam followed into its cavern. The "United States," the "Boardman," and other vessels of the squadron,

come up. The fine band of the Forty-first, on the
"North Star," play, "Twinkling stars are laughing,
love," and other pieces, to the delight of all the transports. One of our fellows offers to "swap our band
for yours;" which goes for a great joke aboard the "Illinois," we being rather lame in point of music,—a few
drums and fifes, with a most limited *répertoire* of tunes.
A certain creeper, the pest of camps from time imme-
morial, has made its appearance on the "Illinois," as
was to be expected; and been the staple horror of the
latter part of the voyage. Of course, some one must
yell out the inquiry, if the Forty-first know any thing
about them. The answer comes pealing back across the
water: "We've got 'em with U S. marked on their
backs." So go the jokes through the evening.

Dec. 15.— Morning comes after a night almost
sultry. The air is dead; and, although the stateroom
window has been wide open, we all awake in a perspiration. Daylight drags the wolf out of his cavern,—
the city out to view. We find we are rather below it;
opposite a pretentious building, which, I believe, is the
Marine Hospital. In the course of the morning, we
weigh anchor, and sail up a mile or so; the straight
streets opening up as we go slowly by, looking quiet,
and, with the wharves and buildings along the Levee,
forsaken by business. We pass the Cathedral; a fine
structure, so far as I can see, with a square in front,
and two buildings of a mediæval appearance on each
side, — convents, perhaps; then long sheds and mar-
kets. At length we are opposite the Custom House,

— which has the revenue-flag flying, — an uncompleted building of Quincy granite, which, they say, was proving too heavy for the soil, sinking downward, until they were forced to stop building.

Here are the great peace-keepers of the city. After passing two French war-steamers, we come to frigate after frigate, grim, dangerous, silent, our flag at the stern; with formidable batteries, all in perfect trim, and trained straight against the city. Blue tars crowd the decks; watchmen, with spy-glasses, are in the tops. Should secession grow rife again, and, in city or suburb, the watch behold the dust arising from an *émeute* which the soldiery could not repress, New Orleans would be blown into shreds and splinters. We cast anchor again. As the day goes by, we buy oranges, ripe and sweet, from boats which come alongside; while the hope of being landed during the day, held out in the morning, fades and fades.

CHAPTER III.

THE TWO LEADERS.

DEC. 16. — I am writing now among the great columns of the St. Charles Hotel, in New Orleans, in front, detailed for special duty at head-quarters, in a clerkship which Gen. Banks offered me this morning, and which I have accepted on trial. It will give me a place close by the general, and, I hope, a good opportunity for observation and to be useful. I left the ship last evening just at dusk, thinking I would settle the matter at once, — wait upon the general, present my letters of introduction and credentials, and see what he would do for me. The "Illinois" had hauled up to shore. I loaded my revolver, climbed down the wheel-house, and made my way up through the streets, toward the St. Charles Hotel, to seek my fortune. It was a hostile city : but the sense of insecurity which I had when I landed soon wore off ; for people were invariably polite when I made inquiries ; and, had they not been, soldiers of the Union passed me at every few rods ; and not unfrequently I came upon sentinels posted in doorways, on sidewalks, before places of amusement. Occasionally I passed buildings which seemed very fine in

the dusk; and at length the stately front of the St.
Charles threw its glare over me, as I ascended through
the gas-light into the rotunda. Shoulder-straps were
innumerable among the tall columns, — double-breasted
colonels and majors, with eagles and leaves, — and
slimmer captains and lieutenants, with the single row
of buttons.

The general was not in : so I was forced to wait until
this morning, though I ran the risk of losing the "Illinois," which might sail any hour, leaving me with my
fate undecided. Soon after eight this morning, fortified with a good breakfast, I went again to the St.
Charles. The general was at breakfast. I sent in
my name on a card, with my documents, and waited.
In half an hour, perhaps, an unpretending figure, in
blowze and loose pantaloons, with felt hat and shuf-
fling slippers, crossed the marble floor just in front of
me. At first, I did not notice him. His appearance
was less *distingué* than that of the least second lieutenant among the columns; in fact, I believe even the
corporal outshone him in his freshly brushed dress-coat.
As he passed opposite me, however, I saw it was the
general going to his rooms.

He is out of sight now, and I wait to be summoned.
Wait, wait. If he comes out again, I determine to
waive ceremony, and present myself. Here he does
come! Up, courage, before he is swallowed by shoulder-
straps! I touch my cap, give my name. He is very
polite, — "was looking for me;" and I presently feel at
my ease. The iron-gray moustache over the mouth is a

grim and formidable archway, but from under it proceed pleasant words. At present, he can only offer
this clerkship. I may take it, and wait for something
better to turn up. He leaves me to think about it;
meantime inviting me into his parlor, where I sit among
eagles and stars, who come and go.

Colonels of regiments just arrived are here to report.
Major Varnum reports : —

"I am paymaster, sir. I have brought with me a
million dollars."

"Indeed!'" (the general, with a pleasant smile and
imperial bow :) "then we are all glad to see you,
major."

"Major So-and-so is coming with eight hundred thousand dollars more."

"Ah! then we shall all be glad to see him, — almost
as glad as to see you."

The general withdraws. I make up my mind then ;
take out my paper, and read, while the adjutant-general
and his clerks (who occupy this parlor for the time
being) write and write. The general appears again,
walks across the room, his hands behind him, and face
bent down, in deep thought. He is just about to meet
the municipal authorities of New Orleans, — an important interview. As he approaches my corner, he looks
up, and smiles affably I tell him briefly I will come
on trial, — not to stay unless I choose. I am then introduced to the adjutant-general, and presently retire
to the shadow of these great columns of the portico :
but, before I go, I behold the general in full blaze, —

double star on each shoulder, double row of buttons in front; the sash of his office about his waist, which the adjutant-general steps forward and adjusts. As I pass out, the civic dignitaries are entering, — a body of gentlemen of good bearing and substantial aldermanic appearance.

I have also an opportunity, just at night-fall, to contrast the setting with the rising sun. In the afternoon, I pass the handsome mansion occupied by Gen. Butler as his head-quarters. From the stoop I am hailed by name, and look up to behold Callighan and Pat O'Toole of our company, who have got lost, and come to the guard, before the door here at head-quarters, to be set straight. I go up on to the roomy stoop; and, as we stand talking by the sentry, two gentlemen come from within to the door, escorted by a third with portly figure and thin hair. It is the verge of evening, and I cannot see his face plainly. "Shall we say at half-past four, then?" It is Gen. Butler, making an engagement with his visitors for the next day. He goes in. I hear a door close, and through the blinds I can see him in an elegant parlor, alone, reading; the gas-light falling full on his large frame and rather sinister face.

Dec. 19. — In camp, within the memorable town of Baton Rouge. My clerkship at New Orleans was short-lived. I found my associates were to be very coarse men. I was to rub constantly with commissioned officers (many young and thoughtless, many of them high in rank), among whom, in my position, it would be hard to feel independence; and I might be

subjected to treatment hard for a man of any spirit
to endure, however Christian he might endeavor to be:
all this in a strange city, with not a soul to go to for
congenial companionship. I slept at night in a room
appropriated to the head-quarters' clerks, half filled up
with a litter of confiscated furniture. Rising early, I
packed my knapsack, and saw my superior as soon as
possible; not to report for duty, but to tell him I preferred to remain with my regiment.

New Orleans I found a pleasanter city than I expected. Many streets have fine blocks, and a few
buildings are really handsome. The business of the
city must have been immense; though now, in thorough-
fares lined with stores, and once, evidently from the
look of the pavements, thronged with passers, one's
foot-step echoes hollow from deserted buildings. I
was treated with invariable politeness when I came into
contact with the inhabitants; though I wore my loaded
revolver under my coat, and slept with it under my
pillow, not knowing what might occur. On St.
Charles and Canal Streets, I saw some of the ladies of
the city, — at least, so I judged from their dress and
faces, — but there was nothing insulting in dress or
manner; and I was informed that demonstrations of
that character had long since ceased. Many of these
ladies were in deep mourning, probably for relatives
killed in the Confederate service.

One needs to have a long purse in New Orleans. I
believe this is always the case, but especially now, when,
the river being closed, the city depends solely upon its

environs and the sea for its supplies. Even the fruits,
which we expected to procure very cheaply, cost as
much as in New York, though orange-trees and the
banana, with its heavy plume-like leaf, grew in almost
every garden.

I proved it to be true, that there is no loneliness like
that of being alone in a great city, full of strangers;
and was as happy as I care to be, when I found I could
depart.   The "Illinois" had left, and, as I found out,
had gone with the regiment still further up the river, —
to Baton Rouge.   I was to take a river-steamer, the
"Iberville," chartered by the Government, and about to
carry up the river the famous Second Massachusetts
Battery, Capt. Nims, which first became noted at this
very point of Baton Rouge, in the battle of August,
1862.   I bought some oranges, got my knapsack off
with the help of a brother-corporal of the battery, and
took my seat on the forward deck, just over the hubbub
of the embarkation, to see the polished pieces, the fine
stout horses, and the heavy caissons of ammunition.
In this battery, the orders all are communicated by the
bugle ; whose call, horses as well as men understand.

I sit on deck beneath a June-like sun.   A crowd
have assembled on the Levee ; in large part, of contrabands.   Boys cry the papers with Gen. Butler's farewell.   My oranges are delicious ; more sweet and ripe
than we get them North.   Behind me, in the river, lies
the "Hartford," with Admiral Farragut on board ; the
"Mississippi," "Pensacola," and the smaller gun-boats.
In the distance, down stream, lie the two French war-

ships, and the "Rinaldo" flying the cross of St. George. Up stream lies a steamer with the flag of Spain, — swarthy watchmen on the paddle-boxes, the space over the forecastle crowded with sailors of the same hue. There are but few merchant-ships, and little appearance of commercial bustle. Big artillery-men (artillery-men always look strong), Boston boys in red-trimmed jackets, wheel the light cannons aboard the ship. These shining pieces are no dainty holiday affairs, that never go out of arsenals except on Fourth of July or after an election, and then only belch harmless discharges. Each one, on the average, has probably killed its score of men, and wounded perhaps two or three times as many. Smooth, elegant, polished, quiet, they stand on deck like elegant French swordsmen I have read of, who go with dainty rapiers, almost plaything-like, soft as silk, but dangerous as death.

By sunset, horses, men, and all, are aboard. Callighan and O'Toole are safe at hand, glad as I am to go to the regiment. The boat swings out just as Gen. Banks is leaving the "Hartford" from a visit of ceremony. His boat shoots forth rapidly, rowed by eight skilful oarsmen; and from the ports of the "Hartford," now one side, now the other, roars the appropriate salute of thirteen guns, the tremendous report making the light scantling upper works of the steamer I am on quiver like jack-straws.

We are moving rapidly up stream, the city under its guard, the closed stores and crowd of negroes going rapidly behind, while sugar plantations on both sides

come into view above. Battery-men tell stories of the
Baton-Rouge fight, — how this one had a horse shot under him, and that one had a man killed at his side. As
evening closes, the horizon before and behind is lit up
with immense fires, consuming the dried and crushed
stalks of the sugar-cane. Pat Callighan and their
" co-r-r-poral " sit under the stack on deck, the evening
being cool ; while an Irish sergeant of the First Louisiana, who has served in India, tells stories of the skill
of the Sikhs at Sobraon and Chillianwallah.

Before daylight, the boat is at Baton Rouge. I roll
out of my blankets on the cabin-floor, and go ashore.
Climbing up the Levee, and finding there Company D
just finishing breakfast, having slept on their arms all
night, I feel happy enough to be once more among the
fellows ; and throw my knapsack down by Ed.'s, in one
corner of a tent, with much more satisfaction than I
should have taken in a carpeted parlor in New Orleans.

I hear of the warlike experiences of the day before.
It seems that the transports (several of which were in
company after leaving New Orleans) followed one
another in close line, protected by gun-boats. During
the night, which soon fell, word went out, that, the next
day, there would probably be fighting. The rifles were
got out of the boxes in the hold, loaded, and each man
supplied with forty rounds of cartridges. There was
some anxiety in the regiment (for we are almost entirely
lacking in musket-drill), but, I believe, no unmanly
fear. By morning, the ships were opposite Baton
Rouge, held by a body of the enemy. The famous

iron-clad " Essex " appeared, to re-enforce the squadron.
Some twenty shell were fired, mostly by the " Essex ; "
the Fifty-second, for the first time, having the opportunity to hear the booming of guns of large caliber and
the whistle of projectiles. The enemy retired immediately ; whereupon our troops were at once landed from
the transports, and posted within certain old intrenchments. These were thrown up last summer by Gen.
Williams, and run zig-zag through the town, without
respect to buildings, streets, or graveyards.

CHAPTER IV.

"THE DAY OF CLOUDS AND THICK DARKNESS."

JAN. 19.—One by one, all the phases of military life are passing before me. Camp and transport life I know,—picket and guard duty, and the routine of drill. For a month, this has been our life,—a tedious and uneventful season, whose incidents it is idle to record. The battle-field, so far, has kept aloof with its bloody terrors; but now I am face to face with a chapter of the soldier's life, less hideous than the battle-field perhaps, yet full of sadness. Suddenly I come to see hospital-service; and, as I feel to-night, it is quite possible I may see much of it: for while there is so much sickness in the regiment, and I continue well, perhaps I can best employ myself in nursing. I am writing here at ten at night, in what the doctor calls my "ward;" a pleasant, airy chamber belonging to the officers of our company, who, however, with great kindness, have given it up to Ed. and Sergeant Grosvenor, who lie here sick of fever. I snatch the intervals between the calls of my two patients to write. Two of our men sleep here on the floor, who are to watch part of the night. It will be an hour or two before I go to bed; and I may have an opportunity to write a good deal.

My first visit to the hospital put me face to face with its gloomiest spectacles. A mail had come, and it fell to me to distribute to the patients their letters. I had been giving letters to well men, had my own pocket full, was happy myself, and had come from among men happy as men ever are; for I have discovered the secret of happiness to be hidden in mail-bags. I rushed up the stairs leading to the second story of the building, the rooms of which are used as part of the hospital. Two or three doors were before me. I opened the first, and found myself alone in the presence of a corpse. It was the body of a man who had died the night before. He lay in full soldier's dress, decently brushed coat with military buttons,—his "martial cloak around him,"—and with a white cloth covering the face. He was buried in the afternoon; the regiment drawn up in a hollow square, solemnly silent, while the service was performed; then standing reverently while the body and its escort with the muffled drum moved to the burial. I have heard of the "wail" of the fife, but never made it real to myself until then, when across the parade-ground, down the street, then from the distance, came the notes of the "Dead March."

In the next room to the one in which lay the corpse, the floor was covered with pale, sick men. Now they have rough bedsteads, "bunks;" but then there was nothing but the mattress under them, and sometimes only the blankets. One or two attendants, as many as could be spared from the regiment, had the care of the whole; but they were far too few. One poor man was

3

in a sad way, with inflammatory rheumatism, which
made it very painful for him to stir; and, at the same
time, with dysentery, so that he required to be lifted
every few minutes. Pale, forlorn men, away from
friends, tended by nurses who have no special interest
in them, and are overworked, — crouching, wrapped up
in blankets over the fire, or stretched out on a floor.
God pity the world if it has sights in it more melancholy
than a military hospital!

The hospital of our regiment is only in part located
in these rooms, of which I have been writing. Most
of the patients (I am sorry to write, they are very numerous) are in a larger building, once a hotel, which
lies a few rods outside the lines. Well do I know the
road thither now, by night or day, by storm or sun-
shine; for, after the doctor's visits, it is my work to go
to the hospital-steward after the medicines and comforts
for my sick men. How many times already have I
climbed the steep clay bank of the parapet, then slid
down into the ditch outside! — a hill of difficulty in bad
weather, when one's feet slip from under him in the
slimy soil. The old bar-room of the hotel is now the
hospital-kitchen and head-quarters of the surgeon and
steward. Above the bar is a flaring gilt sign, "Rain-
bow Saloon;" and below it, along the shelves which
once held the liquors, are arranged the apothecary
stores of the regiment. The steward is constantly busy,
— one of the hardest-worked men in the regiment, I
believe; for he prepares pills and powders by the thousand, and the rattle of his pestle is almost constant.

In the rooms above lie the sick men, and in one apartment the surgeon is quartered.   Every morning, just at
light, "surgeon's call" is beaten ; and from each company a sergeant marches off at the head of a long line
of sick men to be prescribed for.   These are men unwell,
but not so badly off as to be obliged to leave their ordinary quarters for the accommodations of the hospital.

Let us go up stairs into this second story.   At the
head of the staircase, the door of a room is ajar ; and I
see the bed on which generally is lying one of the sick-
est patients of the hospital, some man near to death, —
a comfortable, canopied bed, a death-bed for numbers.
To-night, poor Paine, of our company, who died a
little while ago, has just been laid out there.   An
entry runs north and south, from which, on each side,
open the doors of other sick-rooms, where men with
fever and dysentery, with agues, and racking, lung-
shattering coughs, lie stretched on mattresses.   Here is
one with ghastly fever-light in his eyes ; there, one pale
and hollow-cheeked.   Wrapped to the chin in blankets,
some are ; some parched with the fire of disease, —
their buttons and gay dress-coats, the finery in which
they used to appear at dress-parade, hanging forlornly
overhead.

The nurses, too, look jaded and worn : and no wonder ; for, with a dismal contagion, the torpor and weari-
ness in the faces about will communicate itself to the
attendants and visitors, and the most cheerful countenance can hardly help becoming forlorn.   Our chaplain
and colonel (both good, energetic, and useful men)

make it part of their daily duty to go to every couch, and befriend the poor fellows lying there; and their visits are the golden hours of the day at the hospital, — waited and prayed for. The doctor's apartment is large. In one corner are piled up the " stretchers," the cots with handles (half-bed, half-bier), which are meant to carry wounded men off the field. At daybreak, each day, this room is filled with the procession which answers the surgeon's call.

Now I am a nurse in the hospital; though in the room, my " ward," I have only two patients, and can make things more comfortable than in most of the rooms. Only two patients : but they both have this terrible fever; and I fear (God knows how much!) for this young brother. Yet I must veil my apprehension. To-night, a letter must be sent North. My heart is sinking; but I must counterfeit light-heartedness, lest they take alarm.

To the Parsonage in B.

DEAR P., — We are lucky fellows. For a time, you know, Ed. and I were perfectly well and hearty; and, now that Ed. has had to give up for a while, he is probably better off than any sick man in the regiment, and is doing as well as we can expect. I wrote a day or two ago, that Ed. was sick; thinking he would be better at once. It turned out differently; and now he is slipping smoothly through a fever, — just about as comfortably off as he needs to be, with every thing so far going well. It does seem at a distance an awkward thing to be sick in camp, and generally, I suppose, it is a hard thing for a soldier to be taken down; but Ed. is singularly fortunate. The chaplain offered him a place in his room, which he thought would be more comfortable than the hospital; but the officers of the company were so urgent in their invitation, that Ed. decided to go to their room. So here we are to-night, — he playing patient; and I, nurse.

Grosvenor is sick too, — fine fellow, — the graduate of Amherst, whom I mention sometimes. He and Ed. have the room together; and the colonel has detailed me temporarily for hospital-service, to have special charge of this pair of sergeants. You know I am an old hand at nursing. I find I take to it again with real zest, like a fish to its pond. Ed. and Grosvenor are both sleeping quietly now, each on his bunk comfortably fitted up with a soft mattress of moss and all necessary coverings. The surgeon is skilful, and close at hand all the time; the hospital-stores contain all the necessary medicines; and, for comforts, you ought to see the pile of oranges and lemons on this table here! Oranges, not such half-ripened, pale fellows as you see North, but the "*raal*" article, pumpkins in color, and almost in size. Ed. has just been smacking his lips over some cold lemonade sucked up through a mint-julep straw, and is looking forward to beef-tea; a cupful of which, nicely made as can be by old Winders, the hospital cook, who takes an interest in us, stands on the bench yonder. Moreover, there is toast-water, fine loaf-sugar, choice tea, right here at hand, and gruel whenever it is wanted. Ed. sleeps on a feather pillow which I managed to get; and, as I said, sucks his nourishment through a mint-julep straw: not because he is obliged to, but because he prefers to take it easy, — lie flat on his back, or any way, and take his dinner, which, under the persuasion applied by means of the mint-julep straw, will pliantly mount any hill, or turn any corner, to find that "right spot" to which we like to have things go exactly. So you see Ed. is about as well off as he could be anywhere, all things considered; and, in some respects, better: for he has the *mint-julep* straw, — an article which savors of the "enemy," and which, therefore, never *did* profane, and I presume would never be *allowed* to profane, the virtuous precincts of the manse; and yet an article (O our friends!) to be cherished for its magic mastery over lemonade and beef-tea. So you see Ed. is well doctored and well nursed. I am not afraid to say it. For myself, my health is perfect; and I take precautions to keep it so, so far as I can.

Ed. has waked up. He sends much love, and talks about Mark Tapley, the "jolly man;" who, when he was too sick to speak, wrote "jolly" on a piece of paper. That appears to be about his frame of mind.

BATON ROUGE, Jan. 26.

DEAR P., — This evening is really the first time when fatigue and work give me some respite, and I can begin to give you the sad particulars, — how our much-beloved

Benjamin went from earth into the bosom of the Father.
Tears and convulsive sobbing are now over with.   I
am calm, as I begin; and perhaps I can go through the
detail with the gathering of no film and the trembling
of no nerve.   I am left here forlorn; my pride and joy
taken from my side.   It is evening now.   I still am in the
house where he died, — a deserted house now; its only
tenants to-night being Robert Bodwell (the good fellow
who helped me nurse him) and I.   We are not in the
room where he died, but just across the hall, in the
chamber where we went after we had laid him out, that
we might watch close at hand, and yet not intrude upon
his solemn sleep in death.   The clouds are dark, and
the wind blows damp and chill from the northward,
across the fresh turf upon his grave, then against these
shutters.   The last duty now is done.   In the centre
of the floor stands the box in which I have packed his
things, — knapsack and cap, clothing and canteen, and
soldier's blanket, — all worn and marked as he wore and
marked them; but they will be all the more precious
for the stain upon the woollen, the hole in the garment,
the rust upon the blade.

The first complaint of sickness which he made, I remember, was a fortnight ago this very day.   We were
ordered to stand under arms an hour before breakfast.
It was raw and dark; and the companies, shivering and
with empty stomachs, were severely drilled.   I recall,
that, when he came in, he sat down, — the new morning
light showing his fatigue, — and said, "It was too much
for him : the double-quick caused nausea, and almost

made him vomit." Still, through that day he was
about his work, as usual, — at every drill, and calling
the roll at night by his lantern's light, wrapped in his
blue overcoat. Tuesday he was too sick for duty. He
complained of weakness and dizziness whenever he
attempted to stand; but his spirits were good, and I
never imagined it could be more than a temporary
illness, he has been so constantly well, — "the stoutest
fellow in the company," as they said when he was sick.
He lay still on the floor of the tent all day, — he and
Sergeant Grosvenor, who was sick in the same way, —
his rifle just at his head, polished, and ready for service;
his constant companion, but henceforth to know him no
more, except during one brief half-hour, when, in the
midst of the uncovered and weeping regiment, it lay,
with his belts and crimson sash, upon his coffin-lid   I
remember he was full of jokes even then; and I did
not notice, as others did, that his cheek was unhealthily
flushed, and his breath too short. At night, as we lay
side by side, I threw my arm around his neck, and remember now how hot and dry his face was, and how
short his breath. Hannum, who is an experienced
nurse, startled me in the morning. He thought Ed.
might have a fever. He was plainly sick, and our
company-officers sent for him to come at once to their
quarters. That Wednesday morning, Ed. and I together left the tent, came slowly along the pleasant
river-bank, with the plantations beyond, — his last little
walk on earth, — climbed the stairs, and crossed the
threshold of the room now so hallowed.

Daily he became weaker and weaker. He was soon unable to raise himself; and when, in the afternoon, the fever ran high, and it was time to bathe him, it was hard work to push up his solid young shoulders till he sat upright, and then hold him propped against my breast till he was arranged. Then the heat of the fever! I would pass the cloth, wet with cooling spirit, over his skin; and presently it would flame with red, as if, poor boy! his life within him, beleaguered by disease, threw out the crimson hospital-flag to win forbearance. He became delirious too, though not often wildly so; sometimes calling the company to "fall in," sometimes crying out "to save the colors," as if in battle; and I remember, too, he talked of all of you. Still, there was less of delirium than stupor. His hearing and sight grew dull, and his mind apathetic: yet I believe he always knew me; and he showed a touching confidence that I would do just what was best, which started the tears more than once.

The morning of the day before he died, I thought there was great improvement. His mind was clear, and he had passed a quiet night without an opiate. His pulse, I thought, was slower and stronger; and I moved about him light-hearted. He asked again and again to be bathed. He was not very feverish; but the doctor had told me to let his inclinations guide me: so at length I yielded, and gave him a bath. Robert and I had found a bedstead in another room, broader than his bunk, which I thought would be so much more comfortable for him, that we took it. After his bath, he seemed so well, that we moved him to his new bed. Then I tucked him in all clean and sweet, ready for the doctor's visit; feeling sure there would be encouragement. Ed., however, now began to show great exhaustion; and, when the doctor came, there was an ominous silence. I feared we had done too much, with the bathing and moving: but the doctor made light of them, saying he had seen some symptoms, the night previous, of a tendency to congestion of the lungs; which symptoms he now found much more marked. After the doctor left, Ed. grew rapidly more weak, until, in my alarm, I sent for him again. He made use, at once, of violent tonics and stimulants, — quinine and brandy, — and had recourse to that expedient which always seems to me so desperate, — chest-blistering. We wrapped his feet, too, in cloths soaked in mustard-water. The extremities began to grow cold and clammy, and I felt that the dear boy's hours were numbered. I went out a few minutes for the air, and wandered helplessly along the river-bank, overwhelmed with agony, — he sinking away from me into a gulf; and, though I reached and yearned after him with all my love, it was no chord that could support him or draw him back to me. About noon, the chill and torpor in which he had lain some hours gave way to fever and delirium. He laughed and shouted wildly with the crowd of phantoms who came trooping to him in his morbid dream, and clutched convulsively at the coverlid. While Ed. had been sinking, Mr. Grosvenor had been recovering; so that now both Robert and I could be

constantly at his side. We gave him cooling drinks,
and the powerful medicines the doctor had prescribed.
Ed. showed no sign of pain ; and, though delirious,
recognized us when we spoke to him. His voice continued to have its strong, vigorous sound. I could
hardly control myself sufficiently to keep at his bedside ;
but I choked back my grief. There was still hope : he
was young and strong, and might, after all, rally ;
but his breathing was very bad, and his galloping heart
could not keep its pace without soon being exhausted.
In the evening, a friend I could trust came in, and in-
sisted I should go to bed while he took my place ; pro-
mising to call me if there should be any change. I lay
down in this room where I am writing now, just across
the hall from his chamber. Once or twice in the night
I woke up, and could hear his voice, strong and firm,
through the closed door.

The morning of the fatal Saturday, Jan. 24, came
at last. I was in the room, refreshed by my night's
rest, at seven o'clock. "I am glad to see you again"
was his greeting, spoken very earnestly. He was pale
and wasted, though his eye and countenance had the
old natural look. I lay down at his side, with my head
by his pillow ; a post I hardly left, except to give him
medicine or nourishment, until the last. About eight,
the doctor came, but saw little change from the night
previous. He continued the same treatment, and still
had hope. Ed. was uneasy, but in no apparent pain.
He would ask to be moved or lifted, or suggest something he thought might give him comfort ; but, if it was

impracticable, he would give it up, yielding most sweet-ly and tenderly to every suggestion of mine. "Oh! never mind; just as you say," with a softness and trust in his tone and look, I cannot think of without a sob.

And now ten o'clock was approaching. I had thrown open the windows and blinds to receive the summer air of the day. The sun was just veiled by white vapor, the river flowed calm and full, and the sound of bugles and bands came in from the camps a mile away. I lay at his side as before. Mr. Grosvenor, a fine man and full of sympathy, now convalescent, sat before the fire with Robert. The sick man became more quiet, and his breathing changed. The hand of death was upon him. I hastily put a cup of brandy to his lips, which he swallowed with difficulty. I sent Robert at once for the doctor; and he had hardly left the room when the dear boy's spirit went upward. There was no agony or spasm; one or two short, quick breathings, and all was over, — the minute-hand just pointing to the second minute after ten.

He went from earth calm in mind, and composed, — painless, fearless, hopeful to the end. He sent you no messages of love. I wish it had been otherwise; but the angels' arms were around him ere we were aware. After all, perhaps it was as well there should be no parting pang, — no disappointment as his hopes fell; though I believe he would have faced his fate with all his noble courage, and with high faith and trust.

A short paroxysm of grief, and I was calm enough to go forward with what was to be done. The chaplain came in, full of the sympathy of a brother; so the doctor. An experienced nurse came over from the main hospital. I bathed the straight, sinewy limbs for the last time. We clothed his tall figure in the familiar soldier's suit, — the brave young limbs and shoulders in their own loyal blue. I wiped his lips and cheeks, and smoothed his locks. I took from his finger his little ring. Presently the coffin came. I helped to bring it up stairs and lay it by him. The captain came in, and paid his tribute of tears above the corpse of his old right-hand man; then he, I, and a fellow-sergeant, lifted him gently; put his blowze, covered with a white cloth, for a pillow; then laid him tenderly in his coffin; smoothing softly his garments; brushing with reverent care every speck of dust away; putting in view his sergeant's badge, — the diamond trebly underscored, — to which office he did honor.

As the day wore on, I went to the burying-ground, where lie the dead soldiers of our regiment, to choose the best spot for him. The ground lies a few rods east of the old United-States Arsenal Buildings, and was once a cemetery of the city, though now it is used for the interment of soldiers. Five or six fresh graves lay in a row, — Roberts, Thomson, Culver, and last our own Paine; large, high mounds, and at the head an oaken board with name, regiment, and date. The row begins near the fence, and runs northward. The fence is of wood, thickly covered with a climbing rose; a dense, luxuriant, beautiful vine, full of bright-green leaves, with the seed-vessels still remaining from the former blossoms.

It wraps the palings so they can hardly be seen; then droops over upon the ground, and spreads its tendrils toward the soldiers' graves. Just over the fence, outside, stands a thick, venerable tree (beech, I believe), whose limbs are swathed heavily with the funereal gray moss. From the foot of the graves, the ground goes downward in a rapid slope. The spot has not the beauty of a cemetery carefully cared for; but it is not unlovely. Perhaps it is not inappropriate, that a short distance off runs the line of intrenchments, through embrasures in which silent cannon watch day and night. I chose for the grave a spot left vacant close by the fence, where the vine could droop directly over it, and the rose-leaves could fall upon it, and the tree, with its mossy harps, could pour its sighing requiems above it. I marked the spot; and Sergeant Hannum, with four who loved him, presently had dug his resting-place.

The funeral was to be on Sunday, at noon. I sat, in the evening of the day he died, with Robert, when presently came steps on the stairs; then Capt. Morton, with Sergeant Warriner and Arthur Sprague, both fine singers, came in. They knew him, as the whole regiment had known him; and Capt. Morton, to do him honor, tendered the escort of his company, while the other two begged to be allowed to arrange a fine choir with appropriate music. I have not mentioned, that, during Ed.'s sickness, the camp of the regiment had been moved from the river-bank into a wood in the suburbs of the town. The tents had gone from the river-bank, and the officers had left the house; so that, during the last days of his life, Ed. and his watchers in the upper chamber were alone in the house.

Sunday came, fragrant and balmy. The heavens were full of clouds, like angels' wings; no parching heat, but grateful air, inspired with all sweet odors. Spring birds sang in the trees. In solemn calm poured the great river before the windows where he slept. In good time, around the corner of the building, came young first Sergeant Bertram, Ed.'s familiar friend, marching at the head of the escort; all with burnished arms. They halt in front of the house. Bias Dickinson and Henry Morton come up stairs, and help me arrange on his coffin-lid his equipments. Lie there, eagle that he bore upon his broad breast; and there, shining badge with which he clasped his belt; now his well-kept gun, and here the sash and cap. For the last time I smooth his hair, compose his limbs and dress, that he may seem to his comrades truly to lie like a " warrior taking his rest." Now replace the lid, and let eight of your strongest lift the burden.

> " Slow; for it presses heavily:
> It is a *man* ye bear! "

Down the stairway he had climbed a fortnight before, with halting feet, through the garden in front; now into his hearse. His guard of honor stand with arms reversed; half to march in front, half behind; broad platoons of young soldiers, with downcast faces. Across the parade-ground slowly now. How well it had known his vigorous foot-beat! Now through the rampart and the streets of the town, — the bells of the Catholic church meantime tolling for service, — past the frowning penitentiary, into the shade of trees, until, at length, we saw the tents of the regiment. A majestic temple we had brought him to. Magnolias, with broad, rich foliage, ever green, and trees hung with moss, formed lofty aisles with intersecting branches : and within one of these we placed him ; trembling shadows passing upon his pall, his weapons and belts and badges of office lying on the lid. I could not trust myself to look around : but my eye fell upon field-officers, their eyes shaded with their hands ; and from behind me, where our company was arranged, I heard the sound of much sobbing. How have you told me, comrades, that you loved him ! Manly Rogers, happy-hearted Brown and Hannum, his fellow-sergeants, — from you, from captain and all, there is no dearth of sympathy.

The service begins. The chaplain, with a broken voice, reads the selections ; then came the grand hymn, "Mourn not that his kin are far," Warriner and Browning and young Cyrus Stowell and first Sergeant Arms of B. The notes rose and swelled, and mingled with sweet tree-whisperings and the sobs of soldiers. Their voices choked, and they had to wipe the tears away to see the words. "Warriner, let me have your copy." Is it not a grand requiem for a young soldier? —

> "Mourn not that his kin are far,
>   While we lay him in the grave;
> For his *fellow-soldiers* are
>   Loving brothers of the brave.

And his tender mother here
Shrouds him as a warrior thus:
'Tis his country, loved so dear, —
Mother, too, of all of us.

Sleeping soft, the youth shall lie
Calmly here beneath the sod,
Where, a living sacrifice,
He his body gave to God.

Now let martial music sound!
Beat the dead-march for the brave!
Lower him gently in the ground!
Fire a volley o'er his grave!"

And now the prayer is said. Captain, take his arms
and belts. He is through with them. This little bunch
of Southern lilies, fragrant as his memory, I have further
use for. I take them into my hand from the pall.
Now, Grider, the blacksmith, and Prime, stout Pocumtuc farmer, and the rest, take him in your arms again,
and to his hearse. The wail of the dead-march and
the painful throb of the muffled drum! I love him and
magnify him; and it sounds to me like the agonized
heart-beat of the genius of his country who had lost
him. Slow through the glades of the forest: the sun
of noon strikes down, as we reach the street, upon the
shining arms of the escort, and the hundred young
men, the mourners who march behind. Slowly and
tenderly; and now the little hill is climbed, into the cemetery, and the dead-march ceases. Lay him here on this
convenient tomb; the last prayer; then choir of youths,
"Calm on the bosom of thy God." How sweet! how
soft! We have taken off his coffin-lid again: straight
and tall he lies at full length. His head is turned a

little to one side, and his lips wear a soft and natural smile.

> "They that have seen thy look in death,
> No more may fear to die."

His brothers in arms march in order to take the last look : then it is my turn. Beautiful in death ! The ghastliness of the fever is in great part gone. The features are emaciated somewhat, and the mouth rather more compressed than usual, giving to the nose a fine Roman curve ; not enough to be unnatural, and yet wonderfully dignifying the face, — a faint foreshadowing of the fine mien and presence into which the boy might have matured. I know I am showing brotherly extravagance : but now the thought comes to me of the eager youth leading his charge ; and, as heretofore, the passage comes into my mind, from Henry IV I think it is, "I saw young Harry with his armor on ; beautiful as the herald Mercury new-lighted on some heaven-kissing hill ! " Something like that, I believe ; so lithe of limb ; so free and strong and jocund ; a young winged god of the Greeks ! I would rather have had him fall in battle ; but I know him to be just as much a brave martyr to exposure and faithful work in the cause : and hereafter, if conflict is joined, and his old charge come face to face with the foe ; when they stand with steady discipline, and overwhelm assault with rattling tide of fire, — to him be in part the honor, though he lie cold in death ! I have my lilies in my hand, now upon the pillow right here by his cheek, one for each one of us ; then a deep, warm kiss upon the brow, and the leave-taking is over.

They held aside the climbing vine, and lowered him in his grave. Suddenly, at the word of command, a line of shining barrels was levelled over him, then a loud volley, telling through the camps and town afar that a soldier was at rest. Three times it was repeated, sending echoes far over the river and back into the forest to the outmost solitary vidette; then all was done.

CHAPTER V.

SUSPENSE.

AFTER the funeral, I felt much prostrated; but it was best to keep employed. Robert and I kept our familiar quarters, where at night we could be warm and dry: an important matter now; for at evening it grows very cold, and much rain falls. Water was convenient, too, for the washing which it was necessary to do; and I could pack at leisure the things I wished to send North. In a few days, all this was done. I took my farewell of the apartment where Ed. died, now stripped to its bare walls; and, not being quite in condition to go into the woods to camp, I accepted the doctor's invitation, and spent a day or two last week in his private room. In one corner lay the stretchers, ready for the wounded men; in another, a patient sick of fever. By night, I could hear the shouts of the delirious patients from the corridors.

I saw three bodies lying together on the roof of the veranda of the building, overlooking the street. A little breath of air came; and the covering was turned down from the face of one, a member of our company,— his, and yet not his, — a fine fellow, a favorite of Ed.'s,

at whose feet he now sleeps. One of the others be-
longed to us too, — a boy I knew well. He will never
see again his pretty cottage-home under the trees by
the Connecticut. The chaplain was sick the day of the
funeral : so I conducted the service for these two at one
time, after dark, under the moon. We were forced to
bury them hurriedly, for it was late ; and I fear with less
of a feeling of solemnity than we once had at such oc-
casions. I believe it is true, that the edge of sensibility
grows dull through use, even in the case of these sad
experiences. Funerals have been so frequent of late,
sometimes three or four a day, that they lose their im-
pressiveness in part.

Pray Heaven the sickness is spending itself! There
are signs that it is so. It has raged, for the most part,
among the youths under twenty, whose immature fibre
appears to afford more congenial harbor for the pestilence than the frames of the older men. Almost all
the deaths have been among the boys. The death-list
is really not as large as is often the case in camps. We
do not suffer as some Maine regiments are suffering
close by us ; but it is large enough to cast a shadow,
and make us all feel the insecurity of life.

My record has been almost entirely of deaths and
hospitals the last few weeks ; but now let me turn from
these things. We are, after all, not a gloomy set ;
though skies are so dull, and health so uncertain. The
spirits of the men are often high, and there is much fun
going forward. A great character in the camp is one
Tibbs, a fellow with many crotchets in his brain, — too

many for it to remain in a normal, healthy state, — and who really, perhaps, ought hardly to have been passed at the medical examination ; but he is a fellow of infinite jest, and his pranks and sayings keep up the spirits of the regiment.   He has wit ; and when that fails, in his blunt talk, he blunders often into capital hits, hitting right and left, sparing no one, from the colonel down. The other day, a large hollow tree had been cut down, and a group of officers stood looking at the hollow. Tibbs came up beside them, and peered with his queer whiskered face into the hole.   "That's a big hollow, Tibbs," said one of the group of officers.   "Well, yes," said Tibbs ; "and next time we have the long roll, if 'taint full of officers, I guess I'll come here and hide."   By all odds, the most amusing thing I have seen since I became a soldier was Tibbs's parody of Col. Birge, of the Thirteenth Connecticut, a veteran regiment, which often went through its admirable drill close by our camp, and whose commander at such times threw himself with unusual energy into his work.   I heard great laughter and shouting on the parade-ground one morning, and, looking out, saw Tibbs mounted on a very lean and long-eared jackass, which he would cudgel until the animal gave up his obstinacy and went off at an ungainly gallop.   Tibbs was excited by the motion, and roared his orders in all parts of the field.   Now it was, "Close column by division, on second division, right in front !"   Then whack would go the stick, and Tibbs, eager as if in battle, would gallop off to the other side of the field.   "Head of column, to the left !"

"Deploy column on first company!" &c., &c. It was an admirable caricature of the efficiency of Col. Birge, who was always at full gallop, keeping his regiment on the double-quick. Tibbs drilled his imaginary command for some time; when some one, perhaps a sergeant, shocked at the indecorum, started after him at full speed. But Tibbs's time had not yet come. As the pursuer approached, Tibbs's ungainly steed reared and brayed; and, while dodging his heels, the pursuer measured his length in the mud, leaving Tibbs the cavalier, in his shabby uniform, to go on caracoling, and shouting his orders.

Feb. 18. — The edge of the evening; in the hospital. At my feet is the stretcher on which I lie often, when I am here on duty at night. It is a good couch; iron legs at each end; two long, limber poles, of ash, running lengthwise, with canvas between, and the ends projecting into handles. As I write now, old Grimes, the horse-shoer, a convalescent, is talking low, with a sick sergeant, of an old flame of his, Chloe: —

"I swan! she was a pretty one, with curls all down her neck."

"Was they white?" asks the sergeant.

"No: kind o' Morgan."

Certainly, Chloe was a lass to charm a young horse-shoer.

For a wonder, I have a table to write on, — a real marauder's table, — two handsome blinds from some destroyed house, roughly nailed together, and set up on four strips of plank. On the slats stand whiskey and

castor-oil; brown-paper parcels of butter; jelly, and
corned-beef from the sutlers; vials of quinine; sugar,
— all in confusion. I sweep aside part of them to get
elbow-room. It is great to have conveniences. I could
write a whole history; but, in the dearth of battles and
sieges, what can I put down? Nothing but little
accounts of those, who, I hope, some day will fight
battles and make sieges; for sorrow be to the Fifty-
second, if we go straight home from this miserable
inactive camp.

I lean against the tent-pole, having just given Ives
his bath, and quieted the man with the measles with a
pill; and, therefore, am at leisure. Along comes
Cripps, the drummer, with a gridiron of blue tape on
his breast, jumping over the puddles, then stopping for
a little chat. I take an interest in the music. It used
to be none too good, and, according to a sharp friend
of mine, was the original cause of the dysentery in the
camp; but there has been an improvement. I ask
Cripps about a certain little musician in whom I take an
interest; there is so much grace and sprightly rattle to
his rub-a-dub-dub as he marches in the line of drummers up and down before the regiment at dress-parade.
Cripps thinks this individual is a "nice boy," though
lately he has come to grief; having kicked out against
authority, and come to the shame of the "barrel" before
the whole regiment. In Cripps's opinion, however, this
youth, nimbly as he brandishes his drum-sticks, is not
the first artist in his line in the regiment: the tenor-
drum is a good deal of an instrument, and "Hodge is

the man who takes the rag rather. Now, Hodge alone
can make as much noise as all the rest on us put together. Its astonishin', but some of these fellers can't
strike right. 'Taint no drummin' to hit with the sticks
all over the head : you ought to hit right in the middle.
A tip-top drummer won't vary more'n two or three
inches from both his sticks, hittin' right in the middle
of the head." I know Hodge well enough, — a stout,
straight boy. I have noticed the fine rhythm of his
almost invisible sticks, and the measured, vigorous
cadence of his feet as he beats time. There is poetry
about old Tyrtæus, who, six centuries before Christ,
marched with his Dorian flute at the head of the warlike Spartan bands. I believe honestly too, that
Cripps and Hodge in their every-day uniforms, seen
through the haze of a few centuries, might be trans-
formed into somewhat romantic characters. Cripps
says about the fifers, "Some on 'em play plain, and
some on 'em put in the fancy touches; but I kind o'
hate to see a man flourish. Why can't he play straight,
without fillin' up his tunes?" There is practical infor-
mation about music.

Burke said the age of chivalry was gone, when he
heard the French had beheaded Marie Antoinette; an
observation he would have been certain to repeat, could
he have heard the recent remarks of Private Clout.

Scene. — The hospital-tent, of a sunny afternoon;
private Clout, sensible, practical, but somewhat unheroic,
seated on the bunk of Grimes, who has gone out to
take an airing. Attendant, couched in the lair of

Chape, opposite, cleaning gun and equipments, against dress-parade.

Private Clout, loq. : "Heard the new rumor, now?"

"Goin' down to New Orleans, p'raps; or, leastways, can if we're a mind to and the colonel's willin' "

Attendant suggests, if we go to New Orleans, in all probability we shall not go to Port Hudson, about to be attacked. We shall only have to do the ignoble duty of petty policemen, — pick up the little boys who will sing "The bonnie blue flag" in the streets, and the naughty ladies who stick out their tongues at the soldiers. We shall have to go home ignominiously, without honor, without having struck a blow, and almost without having run a risk, except from the weather and climate.

Private C.: "Well, honor! — hem! — don't know much 'bout that; but know this: go to Port Hudson, might get killed, — that ain't comfortable; might get your leg shot off. Putty sure of this, anyhow: if you get hurt, after the first, no one cares about it but your relations. If you hain't got none, like as not you die a pauper. I ain't so fast for going to Port Hudson. Down to New Orleans you get good quarters, good livin', and not much to do. S'pose I'd go into swamps, and where them dreadful careless cannon was pointin' my way, ef I was *ordered;* but I'd rather go where it's safe and easy."

Private Clout is a representative man; very sensible and practical, but somewhat unheroic; not given to illusions; disposed to brush the dust off that makes the patterns on the butterfly's wings, — nothing but dust, we all know, not good for any thing, but too pretty to spare.

The other day a soldier came up to me, holding a strip of board : —

"I want you to carve out Elwood's name on this for a head-board to his grave."

"But, Jim, I never did such a thing."

"Oh! they say you can make letters."

At Camp Miller, for want of something to do, I set to work marking clothes ; and did so much of it, I came to be tolerably skilful. Now, this accomplishment had brought me new work. I said I would try, and took the board. I drew Elwood's name as well as I could ; then carefully hollowed out each letter, until it was done. It was a long and fatiguing task, carving hour after hour : but it was pious employment, — making a memorial, however rude, for a comrade ; and I did it as well as I could.

I have also done one for Ed. I chose my board, as good a one as I could find ; outlined the letters ; then, guarding carefully the knife from any improper slip, I sank the name and office deep into the wood. It was the work of days. And now the piece is being framed into an upright, so that it will be the horizontal piece of a cross ; and it will stand at the head of the dear boy's grave.

Feb. 21. — Suspense, — suspense for ever. Every day we expect news of a movement; but it does not come. They are signalling now; they are signalling

night and day from one of the half-ruined towers of the
capitol, by flag and fire.   The old tower is perfectly
garrulous with the ships and the stations down the river.
Scarcely an hour of the day goes by but I hear volleys
of musketry, the cries of platoons of men as they
charge, " the noise of the captains and the shouting;" for
drill goes vigorously forward.   The streets of the town
are full of armed men.

The other day, I saw Nims's Battery at drill.   The
cannons and caissons are all out.   I pass in front of
the muzzles as they are drawn up, — hard things to
face.   There, as usual, is the bugler, covered in front
with broad bars of red, like St. Lawrence escaped from
his broiling before his martyrdom was completed, — he
is there ; but to-day Capt. Nims does his own bugling.
"Toot, toot," a chain of notes, and away they all go on
a gallop; " toot, toot," now they halt and unlimber;
" toot, toot," off again, by the right flank, swords waving, harness jingling, horses kicking with excitement,
— all done to a little chain of clear bugle-notes.
Prompt they are, as if those notes were linked on in
some way to that great rattling battery; and strong
enough to swing the whole affair right or left, horses,
guns, and all; then jerk each man off his seat, as they
come to a halt, and bring him up standing.   Rather
ungracious business, Capt. Nims, blowing your own
trumpet; but you do it very well.

I write on the cluttered-up table, — the two blinds
nailed together.   Where once, for all I know, some
sweet Southern belle sent glances through the slats,

now the quinine mixture of Private Grimes (accidentally upset) strains through on to the floor.

In hospital-life I see the good and bad side of human nature. There are shirks, — but I believe I know one or two, — foul-mouthed often indeed, and altogether too rough, one would think, ever to be fledged out with angels' plumage. They will go home from here (if they live) to a bed on the straw in a barn-loft, or to a cot in a shanty in the woods, where they are getting out timber for some saw-mill; but, in view of their substantial goodness, I know not why, some night, these surroundings should not "like a lily bloom," as well as the chamber of Abou Ben Adhem, and an angel write them down, as "those who love their fellow-men," near the head of God's list, thoroughly unsanctified though they seem, as judged by all conventional standards.

March 11, Wednesday. — I was sitting in the chaplain's tent Sunday evening, complimenting him on his excellent sermon, which he had just preached in the sutler's tent to a congregation of men sitting on molasses barrels, and boxes of almost every thing. Every moment, a bearded face was thrust in at the door with, —

"When does the mail come?" or, "When does it go?"

Presently in comes the sergeant-major.

"Two items of news."

Complimentary corporal becomes mute. Chaplain turns. Inquirer at the door, or rather flap, of the tent, listens attentively.

"First, the 'Nashville' is taken." (Intelligence received with due patriotic joy.)

"Second, orders to march have come at last!"

We expect to march: but hours go by, days and nights go by; and now here it is Wednesday noon, and we are still at the old ground, — knapsacks packed, canteens filled, rations ready. Our shelter-tents came yesterday. They are simply pieces of cotton, about five feet square, with buttons and button-holes on the sides, so that they can be connected. We are expected to get the necessary stakes from some fence or forest, wherever we may be. Each soldier carries one of these squares of cotton cloth. Four of us expect to go together. At night we shall *button up* our house, and be comfortable.

March 13. — I have retreated to the outskirts of the camp this superb morning, and have mounted a stump, portfolio in hand, to record progress. I hope the general is not "up a stump" about his expedition; but here we still are. We have been under marching orders four or five days. The cause of the delay is said to be disagreement among the generals. It may or may not be that.

But impressive preparations have been made for some monster undertaking. Evenings, sometimes, I have gone with my hospital-pass down to the river-side to see Admiral Farragut's fleet (capable, they say, of throwing four tons of iron a minute). The "Richmond" lies farthest up the stream, whose grim, dark broadside we have become so familiar with. Farther down is the "Mississippi," — powerful, noble old frigate, which I remember being taken to see when I was a young child. She is a Cromwell among the fleet; never doing any thing but peaceful work all through early life on to middle age; then suddenly plunging into fiery warfare, and making an immortal name for herself. Stained and warty and wrinkled is her old hull, as was the face of Cromwell; moreover, painted a shade of gray, so that she looks hoary, — blistered from tropic exposures, scraped and scarred from ice-floes, but stanch yet to the keel, and perhaps the most reliable member of the squadron.

The "Hartford" lies below, whose battery I heard thunder at New Orleans. The "Essex" is drawn close up in shore. I lean against the wheel of a powder-wagon, and look, at my leisure, at her formidable plating; her pipes rising from the hard shell like a pair of snail's horns; the big guns showing their muzzles through the ports, like dogs that want to be petted. To her present fame, what new glory is she about to add? The mortar-vessels are stretched in a line below, and close to the Levee lies the trim gunboat "Kineo."

It is late twilight now. I sit on the embankment, looking at the pale, yellow sky westward, between which and my sight intervene the masts and rigging of one of these mighty gladiators of the deep. She lies far enough distant to make it impossible for me to hear any sounds from her deck, except most faintly; but I can dimly see the back of the great eleven-inch Dahlgren above the bulwarks, — like a saurian crouching upon her deck, — and the watch on the forecastle, — a well-formed, square-shouldered sailor pacing to and fro. Twilight is deepening in the far heavens beyond, — a clear, pale space within a frame of clouds; just the back-ground upon which might be displayed such a heavenly sign as appeared to Constantine of old, — the flaming cross, the harbinger of victory. I see nothing but the bright evening-star, just over the head of the sailor on the forecastle.

Yesterday morning, we thought we were certainly off at last. Word came to be ready to fall in at nine o'clock. Every thing was prepared. I had my forty rounds in my cartridge-box, and twenty additional in my trousers-pocket. For the last, down came the shelter-tent. Bivins packed away his piece, and I mine; and, when the drum sounded, I was promptly with the color-guard. Bias Dickinson is once more at my shoulder. We thought we were off; but we were only to be reviewed. It was as brilliant as one can conceive. Two divisions, brigade beyond brigade; yet Austrian troops in white, or British troops in red, must be more brilliant. Our blue is but a dull hue; yet still ten thousand men together is a sight to behold, — in uniform, in regular formations, — lying long across a field, like wave behind wave, with a foam of bayonets lit up by sun's rays cresting each.

Gen. Banks comes up with a multitudinous staff. Now is the time for splendid steeds, — coursers fitted for an Homeric chariot; the war-horse of Job, his neck clothed with thunder; arching necks, prancing limbs, fetlocks spurning the furrow ; bays, blacks, and grays, prancing and rearing from well-filled bins (for each horse has had his nose in a government-crib). In full dress, in front of the whole, on his coal-black stallion, rides the general. The brigades, one behind another, see him from afar : the brigadiers bring swords to chin, then sweep the point through the air groundward ; banners droop, drums (near and far away) roll a salute. The general removes his cap. He is splendid, — his staff behind him splendid, — glittering with bullion and lace, with buttons and steel. All is splendid ; but the color-guard thinks it is tough work to look at a spectacle in heavy marching order.

Each half-hour puts a new pound into my knapsack ; yet I feel like little Tom Brown when he goes to Rugby for the first time on the stage, riding at night, his legs dangling (too short to reach the support) and tingling in the cold. It hurts ; but Tom finds a pleasure in enduring. It hurts me ; but I find a kind of pleasure. Then, too, I have company enough in my misery ; and do not care much, so long as the sergeant and Bias and Hardiker find it just as hard as I do.

Down the line, on a full canter, now come the general and his brilliant staff. See the bluff captains and commodores from the fleet ! Bump, up and down ! Winnowing the air may be graceful work for the wings of a swallow, but not for the elbows of a commodore. Trip goes a horse into a ditch, and an aide goes down. Down the front of the line, then behind. Then we must march by, — first Gen. Grover, commanding the division, in buff sash and yellow belt, with the division-flag at his side, carried by an orderly, — red field, with a star of white; then the brigadier of the first brigade, with his flag (blue, white, and blue) behind him; then regiment behind regiment, drooping its "good-morning" to the general, in the dipping-colors, as the lines wheel and pass before him, receiving a wave of the cap in return, — horn and bugle, drum and fife, filling the air with glorious sound, — the great host with rhythmic foot-beat moving mightily onward. Now it is over. We march back to the old camp; and, for the first thing, reduce our baggage. We thought, before, we were peeled down to the last rind; but more still must go, or we shall never see Port Hudson. Most of the men resign woollen blankets: but I give up my overcoat; I can spare that best.

The other day I went to Edward's grave, with a spade, to repair and re-turf the mound, which had sunk a little during the rainy weather. This week I have placed the cross, which is to stand at the head. It is simply of wood, painted white, with his name and office deeply carved into the horizontal bar; and, beneath, the date of his death. Of all the soldiers' graves, none is so neat now, in its memorial, in its turf, or location, as his.

They write me, they hope I am still in the hospital; but I am not. There are plenty of invalid or convalescent soldiers, unfit for field-duty, who can tend the sick. I am well able to do soldier's work. If it is God's will, I shall some day go home. The time has come to the young men of this country, when the motto, "Death, or an honorable life." tries more sharply the manhood of him who adopts it than once. Sometimes one can lead an honorable life, and run no risk. I could not be honorable without going into the army. The path of honor for me now is to go with the color-guard into the fire of the Port-Hudson batteries. I would have my life honorable, or go with Ed.

CHAPTER VI.

"INTO THE LION'S MOUTH."

MARCH 14. — On my side, in a corn-field, about thirteen miles from Baton Rouge, on the Port-Hudson road, with Port Hudson from five to seven miles away.   Off for war at last, as sure as we live.   It is the noon halt. Grover's division, far as I can see, lies in lines, one line behind another, in each about one regiment; arms all stacked, with the men behind; some sleeping, some eating, some inspecting feet becoming blistered.   Last evening, we left our old camp in good earnest.   We marched out half a mile to the camp of the Ninety-first New York, with which we are brigaded; then waited for the army to assemble; from street and path a stream of troops, coming like runnels into a larger stream; until at last Gen. Grover himself, with the red flag and white star of the fourth division, went to the head of the column.   A furlong or so in front of us, young Col. van Zandt, our brigadier, took his station with the blue white and blue ensign of the second brigade.   We are all in heavy order, each one of us ὁπλίτης; though, since the review of yesterday, *essential* things have undergone a wonderful diminution; an effective-looking crowd, though not exactly smooth and neat.   We are soon on the point of starting. Our colonel comes riding back from the general, with the resolute, pleasant smile he usually wears, a little more expanded than common. The colonel whispers to Capt. Morton; whereat the captain catches the smile, and he comes back toward his company, — the color-company, you know. "Gen. Grover says the Fifty-second is the best nine months' regiment in the service." A little butter of that sort will help hard fare and tough marching; that the general knows.

Ahead ride the cavalry, yellow trimmings about their collars, yellow welts about the seams of their jackets at the back, and stripes down the pantaloons. Artillery come up. Their trimmings are red; in fine order everybody; horses prancing, cannon polished, muskets in the finest order; an untried army, but of the finest material, and as well equipped, I suppose, as any country through all history has ever equipped her warriors. The march begins, out past the spots where we have stood on picket. I see that the fence-post, against which I leaned all one night, has gone to the coals. We come to two roads branching off from the one on which we are marching: one to Clinton, twenty-five or thirty miles away; the other to Port Hudson. This last road we take. Soon we are beyond the outmost picket-stations, and push forth into unknown regions.

The weather is grand. We are in a heavy magnolia forest: the sun's rays, now nearly level (for it is late in the afternoon), cannot reach us. We go mile after mile. The road is just what it should be, not muddy, not dry enough to be dusty; but smooth and soft enough for the foot to feel it like a cushion, yet not so soft as to take the foot in too deep. It is just wide enough for the regiment to march comfortably by the flank, in sections four deep. Sometimes we go over a hill: then, far ahead and far behind, I can see the big column of infantry, a huge caterpillar eating its way through the woods, jointed along his back where the sections are separated, spiny as a caterpillar's back is, with the hundreds of muskets sticking out at various angles. The night settles down, a night of stars; and from the westward, as the glow fades, rockets go darting up, signals from the fleet, out of sight, in the river, ascending like us, loaded with death against the great fortress. Shall we march all night? No one knows, not captain or colonel, only Gen. Grover apparently; but at eight o'clock, or about that, eight miles on our journey, comes the order to bivouac. A pause in the march, then a quarter of an hour of intermittent progress, then horsemen dimly seen in the starlight; the order to "file right," and I follow the tall color-sergeant over the rails of a destroyed fence into a ridgy corn-field, across which the regiment advances in line, guiding on the centre as well as it can see, then halts; the Ninety-first thirty or forty paces in front, the Twenty-fourth Connecticut about the same distance behind. Stack arms, then camp for the night.

I go back from my place on the left of Co. A to Co. D, and shout through the dark for Bivins. We find a soft place among the furrows: two rubber blankets over a soft ridge make our mattress; then two woollen blankets over; and last the shelter-tents, not pitched, but on top by way of counterpane, to give a finish to the bed. Lie down now, boys, loaded pistol still at the belt, every arm where it can be caught in an instant; for Port Hudson may send out fellows to stir us up during the night. "Corporal Buffum, under the stump there, is your bedroom well aired?" Buffum thinks he shall make out not to suffocate. The night-wind blows over us, the stars shine as only Southern stars do, and in a few minutes fancy runs northward and homeward through a thousand dreams.

The morning comes at last. Is it D or B? The mind gradually gathers itself. Is it the camp by the river, or under the magnolias? Ah! now I have it, — the tall naked trees, the furrows bristling with dry stalks and partially covered with short grass, the army rising like a brimming colony of ants from the ground. Now, as I roll over, my pistol hits me in the ribs, and slap against my legs hits the heavily-weighted cartridge-box. It will make my thigh black and blue, I believe. I have slept as well as I ever did. No one knows exactly when we shall be ordered into line.

At any rate, the canteens must be filled: that is the first thing. Bivins and I draw cuts, and it falls to me: so Cyrus Stowell and I start off, hung round with a maze of white canteen-strings, as if somebody had thrown a net over us. We get back to camp just as the cry "to fall in" is being shouted by the first sergeants. The brigade files out of the corn-field, and is on the road again.

"The thing that hath been, it is that which shall be; and there is no new thing under the sun." I think of that as two companies from the regiment are detailed as flankers. They go off into the woods, fifteen or twenty rods from the road on each side; and throughout the march we see these two lines guarding the main body against ambuscade, — through stumps and stalks, through old sugar-fields, plantation barn-yards, and wild swamps. I remember to have read, that just so Lord Percy, on the retreat from Concord, threw out flankers to protect his harassed party. Probably the children in the houses we are passing, fifty years from now, will tell how Banks went by to Port Hudson, as the old people along the Lexington road recall their great reminiscence.

When I was studying-up the old Assyrians once, I found out that the soldiers of Sennacherib were prepared against the Jewish horsemen with almost the same tactics which the French were to employ against the Mameluke cavalry, ages after, in the same region. So Lord Clyde, in India, once circumvented an army of mutinous Sepoys with the same strategy, particular for particular, which the old Hebrew leader Joshua used against "the men of Ai," in the days when the sun and moon stood still. I dare say, in spite of improvements, we look very much like these old soldiers of the past, as the features of our warfare are similar. In clothing and equipments, we are reduced to what is simply convenient and easy. The pattern of our garments and their quantity, the fashion of weapons and trappings, —

every thing is fitted for convenient use. What is convenient now, was, no doubt, convenient a thousand years ago. Probably, after all, we do not look much unlike the spearmen of Nineveh, the legionaries of Rome, or the halberdiers of Alva, when they put off holiday things, and undertook the active work of war.

The morning deepens toward noon. Fewer soldiers now leave the line to forage among hen-roosts; and the plunder, collected in the cool of the morning, is thrown away as the sun begins to burn. Only the negroes, a half-dozen or so of whom go with each company, stick to their prizes of chickens and turkeys. The Fifty-second grow red, and sweat; and now, along the roadside, we begin to see — what, I believe, is always seen when an army is on the march — knapsacks, sometimes full and sometimes empty, blankets, shelter-tents, all the articles of a soldier's kit, thrown away for relief. Occasionally we stop, when the stream of men rushes from the roadway to the grass at the side, and in a moment every man is flat on his back. It is a good way to rest, though a dirty one: the pack behind supports you at a comfortable incline. Sometimes you sit in the dust, sometimes in the dew: one is not over particular when each pore spouts hot perspiration like a perfect geyser. In one of these pauses, we hear cheering far behind us, that comes rolling nearer; when word passes from mouth to mouth, "The general, the general!" In a moment, a clatter of hoofs, and then past us sweeps the "iron leader," at full gallop and bareheaded, with his staff behind him, on his way to the front of the column.

Men now begin to fall out. They lie panting by the roadside, in fence-corners, under bushes, with heads resting against logs, — a sorrowful sight, though not so bad as if we were on a retreat, and a howling enemy were to pick them up instead of friendly baggage-wagons in the rear. Sometimes there is a momentary hitch as the column picks its way around a mud-hole. I find some relief then for my shoulders in stooping over, and hitching the weight of the pack on to my back. It is robbing Peter to pay Paul; but poor Paul has so much the hardest time, that Peter ought to be willing to give him a lift.

Fortunately, the day is very fine; a grand breeze comes blowing up behind us: it is sunny, but cool; and the vines from the roadside wave white roses at us as we go by, as if the hedges were in for the North, how-ever it might be with the people who lived behind them. Thank fortune! so far as my body goes, it is a good one. Heavy, muscular fellows are pitching away their knapsacks, or lying swollen and panting by the road-side: but, in my case, there is no headache yet; heart works smoothly and healthily in the left side, and liver under the diaphragm; legs swing to and fro without a painful chord, and feet are fully up to their responsibili-ties.

True, it is hard. Whenever the column halts, I am flat on my back, and in the dirt at once. If there is a pool near, I must dowse my hot head, and re-wet the

handkerchief in my cap; but so it is with us all. It is
a good thing, when all favors, to be big and imposing,
like Corporal Green here, and the rest of our fine,
grenadier-looking soldiers; but, for actual work, the
little, light-weighted fellows are even with them.

We have come now some six or seven miles. The
forenoon draws to its close: true as the needle to the
pole, the belly turns dinnerward. The fence is down,
here to the left; and the long column, filing into just
such an old cornfield as we camped in the night before,
rules it across with long, blue lines of soldiery at regular intervals, and proceeds to write it over with such
confusion as some thousands of reckless, hungry men
would be likely to make. Here it is, that, a dried
herring or two and some hard-tack and cheese being
promptly put away, the color-corporal, under the lee
of the stacked arms of the guard, pitches off his traps,
lies down under the folded colors, and writes.

March 18. — In camp on the Bayou Montecino,
between Port Hudson and Baton Rouge. You may
see the place on a large map of Louisiana, — a sudden
bend in the river above Baton Rouge. On Lloyds'
military map, which we happen to have, the bend and
the bayou are both plain.

Bivins and I have buttoned up our house over the
furrows of an old cotton-field: it is open at both ends;
but the evening air is so mild to-night, we can stand
all that.

Our rubber blankets are spread on the damp ground.
The point of a bayonet is stuck in the ground, and in

the bayonet-socket is a candle which gives us light.
The State flag of the regiment, its white silk covered
from the weather, lies along the ridge-pole of the tent.
From the ends of this hang our equipments, in as
apple-pie order as circumstances will permit in a country where there are neither apples nor pie-crust. The
cartridge-boxes are well loaded down with powder and
ball; for rebs of the most truculent sort come down to
within a mile or two of us, and we may hear the long-
roll any minute.

To resume my diary. The Fifty-second had stopped
for its dinner last Saturday noon. I lay, as I have
written it, on my side, pencil in hand; then I snoozed;
then I looked across the furrows, through the sweet,
sunny, blossom-scented air, to the long line of the
Ninety-first, their colors exactly opposite ours. Half
a dozen pigs ran down between the regiments; a gaunt-
let, I believe, not one survived: and before night they
were eaten with much gusto; for, during our stay at
Baton Rouge, we have very rarely tasted fresh meat.

Boom, boom! — big guns from the river. We can
hear, too, the cough of high-pressure transport steamers, and know now that the fleet are, at least, as near
old Port Hudson as we are; and we are only four or
five miles away. At length, "Fall in, men, at once!"
An aide has come galloping up to the colonel, who is on
horseback in a moment. "We shall probably have sharp
work before we come back."—"Keep cool, and do not
waste your fire." So Capt. Morton and the rest give
such caution to their men as is needful on the eve of

battle. "Leave knapsacks here: the footsore men will guard them,"— poor Hines, and the like of him, whose feet these real secesh roads have beaten and bruised with true rebel violence.

How do we feel? We are going out to meet the enemy, we all fully believe, and so do our officers: and even staff-officers of the general, who are friendly to us, look pityingly after, as we march on; for they know, though *we* do not, that we are to be pushed up in front of the whole army, into close range of the cannon upon the fortress-walls. The Fifty-second is cool, and yet eager; and not a man, that can limp at all, wants to stay. For the last thing, "Load!" Open cartridge-box; tear the tough paper from the powder end, — there it goes down the barrel; and now the ball; half-cock, then cap the cone, and all is done. If I have to fire, it will be for the cause. Scruples, now, are mere squeamishness. Now, "By the right flank, forward!" Hardiker carries the white State-flag; the tall sergeant, the stars and stripes. Old flag, you are woven of no ordinary stuff! Rank and file and shoulder-straps, it is a sacred thing! It has for a warp, liberty; and for a woof, constitutional order; and is dyed deep in tints of love and justice. Between Hardiker and the sergeant marches Wilson, — a fine-looking corporal, with a military face, eye, and figure; moustached, bearded, eager; — such a face as I have seen in Horace Vernet's battle-pieces. A good marksman, too, is Wilson; for many years the terror of squirrels in the woods of E——. Prince and Claypole cover Hardiker and Wilson; while I march behind the sergeant, right in the folds of the great flag. Alongside, in the line of file-closers, go West, and lisping, light-haired Wiebel, the German; and, last, the ever sage, serene, and satisfactory Bias Dickinson.

I almost cheered when Bias came back to the color-guard (from which he has been absent for a time, funny fellow!) from the jury-room down at the Court House of Baton Rouge, whilom his headquarters. Did I not dine there once with him, on stewed pigeons? when Bias, a prime confiscator, had got hold of a hand-organ, with which, after dinner, he soothed and gratified his guest by grinding out tune after tune; assuaging the perturbed spirits of the muddy fellow from the camp, as if he were a Saul in all his purple, — an entertainment most gracefully bestowed, with sage, silent, and serene demeanor, and hand turning untiringly at the handle.

So we go out of the field into the road, in the centre of the long column, with banners waving, and, I hope, the true light of battle upon our faces, — soldiers in a noble cause, — farmer and mechanic, merchant and preacher, shoulder to shoulder. "Boom!" go the far-away guns. We are moving rapidly to the front: so the other regiments and the stout battery-men and the yellow cavalry-men give way for us, cheering us on. Down a cross-road toward the river, a sweet south wind shaking white cloud-favors out of every window in heaven at us; the sun smiling God-speed, and the lady rose-bushes, from fence-corners like balconies, showing their blossom-handkerchiefs.

A sweet woodland by-road! We rush forward at double-quick. Ah, here is war indeed!— a colonel on the general's staff, just wounded by the retreating rebel pickets, lying by the roadside. I catch a glimpse of him on an extemporized litter of rails, as he lies under the surgeon's hands. We rush by, tramp, tramp, at the double-quick; and he pushes himself up a little with his hands, so that we can see his pale face, just wounded ahead here in the road where we are going.

Cautiously, boys! A few steps, and we stumble over the handsome horse of the wounded colonel, dead in the middle of the road, with eight bullets through him. There, too, is the bloody boot of his rider, hastily cut off after the wounding was accomplished. A company are detailed as flankers; and, as they go through the wood a few rods distant from the road, they hear the groans of other wounded men. They cannot go to them; for to stop would be to expose the whole flank of the column to danger.

Now we pass other dead horses belonging to cavalry-men, which were shot in the road by the retreating rebel pickets. At length, we reach a fork where is a regiment drawn up, and Gen. Grover sitting on horseback with his staff,— a light-haired man, with face sufficiently resolute, his beard cut in a peak, and wearing a cavalier hat. We halt only for a moment. The general's pointing hand indicates the direction we are to take: so down we go through a wooded road, driving before us the enemy's pickets; our flankers in the woods seeing them mount their horses and gallop off as we come within musket-range.   Presently we go by their camps, where they have cut on trees some defiance or warning to us: "Beware, Yankee! this is a hard road to travel."

By the side of the column rides an officer of engineers, who stops every now and then to note a by-path or prominent knoll, or draw a rough plan of the wood. The dust has hardly settled yet along the road from the tramp of their retreating infantry.   We press on close behind, until at length the column halts close within the range of the Port-Hudson batteries.

It is now just after sunset.   I hitch my cartridge-box a little off my shoulder for relief, and bathe my head and face in a roadside pool.   At the head of the column, spy-glasses are being passed from hand to hand among the officers.   What is it they and the skirmishers see to the northward and westward, from the bend in the road?   If we camp here for the night, we rank and file will go forward to see for ourselves.   They are the outer earthworks of the rebel stronghold.   As the dusk deepens, the column turns, and back we go, — we fellows in the very heart of it; the crimson stripes of the standard leaping and flowing out above us like currents of arterial blood.

We fell back that Saturday night two or three miles, then camped in the woods.   Later, a battery went forward to a position near that to which we advanced, and fired shells for a while toward the rebel intrenchments. Our blankets and baggage were four miles behind.   We hung equipments and haversacks on the gun-stocks;

and, wet with sweat, lay down in our clothes, without covering. Wilson and I laid rails on the ground; then made a sloping roof of rails overhead, which was some protection against the damp.

The eyelids shut together like a pair of scissor-blades, and cut the thread of consciousness; but, in the midst of my dreaming, crash after crash broke upon my ear like the chorus of doomsday. We all jumped to our posts; for we thought the hour of battle had come. I looked at my watch by the light of a few embers. It was half-past eleven. At the time, we were in complete ignorance of the events that were transpiring. We know now that it was the fleet just passing the batteries, and all this was the uproar of the bombardment. Through the trees to the westward arose the flashes, incessant, like the winking heat-lightning of a hot summer evening. Through the air rolled reports, — now isolated, now twenty combining in a grand crash, now a continuous roll of them, — a thundering rub-a-dub, as if the giants were going to storm heaven again, and were beating a *réveille* to summon every gnome and all the genii and each slumbering Titan to fall in for a charge. The centre of the regiment, the color-guard, rested in the road. The pickets, four or five rods off, could see the falling of bombs, the streams of comet-like rockets, and the outlines of the shore-batteries lit up by the cannon-flames. It went on, and we sat listening with our hands close at our guns. Then, at last, the heavens reddened high and far, with a fiercer and steadier glare, that moved slowly southward, crimsoning in turn

5

the moss and old scars on the north, on the west, on the south-west, of the tree-trunks.   Meantime came up the boom of cannon, slowly receding in the same direction. So we heard the swan-song of the stern old "Mississippi," — abandoned, beaten with shot, ragged through her whole frame where shells had torn and burst.   On that night, a freight of dead men were on her deck, and the bodies of drowned men floated about her hoary hull for retinue !   Then came a crash, — a light making all bright, flung back from the burnished gun-stocks, from the pool by the roadside, revealing the watching soldiers and the slain steeds fallen headlong in the road in the midst of the camp.   So passed the veteran ship through fire and earthquake-shock to an immortality in history.

CHAPTER VII.

FALLING BACK.

SUNDAY morning came. We had expected confidently all through the night to be ordered into battle : when light broke, with the dawn, we expected to hear the shots of the advancing rebels. All was still, however. We made fires, and cooked our coffee and beef. I took out my portfolio from the pocket of my blouse, and wrote a sheet or two ; then, finding a clean pool in the woods, I took off every thing, and had a bath. The whole forenoon wore away with no sign of activity. The general was giving us a rest before a very tough march. Toward noon, one of Grover's aides came up with word to fall back. To fall back ! — were we going to retreat, then? Back we go, over the same road as yesterday. As we pass the bridges, we see parties of men, and fuel prepared. " The enemy's cavalry will soon be after us ! " I hear a field-officer say. The bridges are to be burned as soon as we have crossed them. In an hour or two, we are back at the encampment of Saturday noon, passing, as we march, signs of a hasty retreat ; among them, a baggage-wagon on fire. We sling our knapsacks where we left them, swallow a few mouthfuls, and are once more on the road.

We have found out now the loss of the "Mississippi;" and the impression spreads that we have met with great disaster, and are retreating in disgrace. There is no elasticity now, or mirthfulness. It is hard work to carry the knapsacks, and the men are sullen. Retreating without firing a shot!

Yesterday we felt sure of a battle; but the enemy fell back before us. Now, why were we falling back before them? We halt, every half-hour or so; when every one is on his back in a moment. As I noticed the day before, the road becomes strewn with knapsacks and blankets; but fewer men fall out, for they fear capture by the enemy. In the middle of the afternoon, it begins to rain. I never knew it rain so hard: there was a general uncorking among the clouds. The road becomes a deep pudding, and the gutters are rivers. We are wet to the skin. I throw my left arm against my breast-pocket to shield (as much as I can) my portfolio, which has my precious paper and pencils. By great care, I partly succeed; but every thing else is soaked. Boots become filled with water that runs from the clothes into them. The army splashes on through the rain, dreary and disheartened. Some of the officers give up their horses to tired soldiers, and shoulder muskets.

At five o'clock we reach a field, where we are to encamp. Gen. Banks assigned it when he passed in the morning. Since then, creation has put on a new face; but we must obey orders. In we turn, therefore, into a swamp, to pass the most tedious night of our lives.

A dreary Louisiana swamp! The space had been cleared, and was full of charred stumps and logs, half floating, half lying in the mud. There was a terrible exhibition of democratic licentiousness. The rain had been so violent, that the pools — the "lower ten million" — had become multiplied; had out-rooted the little green patches of *terra firma* that held themselves higher; and, with small respect to the minority, were proceeding fast to reduce the whole thing to a lake. We waded and stumbled forward to the middle of this dreary quagmire. Could we stop here for the night? We had marched very rapidly ten or twelve miles, most of the way in heavy order; and were exhausted. The roads were almost impassable : moreover, the general had left orders for us to stay here. We had no choice.

Wet to the skin, I threw off my knapsack and equipments into the mud, too tired to hold them. We managed, as night fell, to get a fire started in a charred stump; then, through the evening (which was dark as pitch), we went stumbling about in the bog, to find sticks for fuel, — fishing out of mud-holes such half-burnt branches and trunks as we could lift. Frequently the rain would pour in sheets; when the fire, in spite of all we could do, would dwindle down to a mere spark.

About ten o'clock, I managed to make a little coffee. Then putting my knapsack into the mud, in the highest and dryest spot I could find, drawing my two blankets about my shoulders, and my rubber havelock over my

ears, I sat down for the night. As I sat on my knapsack, it settled down into the mud until it just kept me
out of the pool. My boots sank into the mud half-way
to the tops. I rested my elbows on my knees, and
chewed the cud of misery. Once in a while, some
one waded forth after wood. On every stump and
log were figures wrapped up in rubber blankets, trying
to sleep. I mistook Silloway, thus enveloped, for
a charred stump, and began to haul him to the
fire; when a feeble and dismal voice proceeded
forth.

Nothing was ever more wretched; and, when morning came at last, — swimming up through the pouring
heavens to us, — such a half-drowned, haggard, bedraggled set as the regiment was, horses and men! We
had the consolation of thinking we had touched the
bottom of misery, at any rate. Any lower deep there
surely cannot be. Snakes and crabs, no proper food
or drink, wet to the skin, the deadly vine weeping its
"venomous dew" upon us, — there could be nothing
farther down. Mildewed, frowzy, horrible!

Still there was a very fair amount of good-nature.
One rather portly officer had tumbled off his log during
the night into the mud, which made a great laugh.
Poor Corporal Wright came to our fire in the morning.

"How are you now, old fellow?"

"Oh! gay and festive, — more than 'How are you?'
It don't express it" (delivered with a feeble and dismal
smile).

There is spunk in the regiment yet. We have scarcely any thing to eat. Nobody wants to eat much of any thing; but the foragers go out.

This matter of foraging is a hard one. I have seen now what a scourge to a country an invading army is. We were turned loose. As I shall presently record, the Government, under our guns, collected a large amount of cotton; and we were suffered to kill cattle, pigs, and poultry. All this marauding went on ruthlessly and wastefully. We left the road behind us foul with the odor of decaying carcasses. Cattle were killed, a quarter or so taken out of them, and the remainder left to the buzzards. So with sheep and poultry. Pigs were bayoneted, sugar-houses plundered of sugar and molasses, private dwellings entered; and, if any resistance was offered by the owner, his arms were wrested from him, and he overmastered. To be sure, there can be no manner of doubt of the sympathy of all these people with the rebel cause. We saw nothing of any young white men, — only old men, negroes, and women left behind by the young men when they entered the Confederate army. I have not heard that any were actually slain in these marauding expeditions, or that insult was offered to any white woman; but property was handled, destroyed, or taken, without scruple.

I took no part in any active foraging, though I own I was more than once a partaker in the booty. It was, in fact, our only way to live. Government-bread and poor bacon were really insufficient to support strength under our work and exposure. When Bias offered me some fine cutlets, Sunday morning, from a calf he had just killed, I took them without much reluctance; and so, when Sile Dibble brought in steaks almost by the armful, and canteens of molasses, and haversacks of sugar, I was glad, hungry and tired as I was, to take the share he offered me. If I did no active foraging, it was, perhaps, more due to want of enterprise, and because there were enough others to do it, than because my conscience stood in the way. Am I demoralized? But it was the only way to live. Our rations were insufficient, and the commissary-department seemed to expect we should find a good part of our food for ourselves. It is, indeed, sad; and there was enough that was pathetic. War is horrible, and this feature of plunder is one of its horrors.

All this had humorous features too. To see Bias knowingly and amiably dissect a stolen calf, was a cheerful sight; so, too, Sile Dibble, mounted on a lean horse which Gottlieb had stolen, careering across the lines with geese and chickens held by the legs, fluttering and screaming, in one fist, and a bag of meal in the other; so Pat O'Toole, our wild Irishman, tearing through the camp, after having shot eight cows, without his hat, screaming to the " bys to eoom afther his coos afore thim spalpeens of batthery-men had tuek thim intirely " These were humorous features; but there was more to grieve over than to laugh about, and I fear it will be thought to speak ill for our New-England men that they take so easily to this habit of " loot."

March 21. — We staid in the swamp through Monday forenoon. At noon came the order to pack up, which was done with thanksgivings; and we waded and paddled out to the road, just as the sun appeared once more through the clouds. We marched, for the distance of about a mile, through a lane running westward; coming, at last, to an elevated field on the river-bank, at the Montecino Bayou, — a pleasant, well-drained spot, — where we camped at once to dry and rest ourselves; the stacks of guns, as usual, running in a long line, with the shelter-tents behind them; the two flags, in their glazed cases, crossed on the middle stack, indicating the centre of the line. The powerful sun soon dried our outer clothing; and, content with that, at nightfall we lay down to sleep; willing enough to postpone, until another day, the drying of shirts and drawers and the contents of our knapsacks.

We had come to a very pretty spot, and in such contrast to the camp we had just abandoned! I remember, Ruskin says, somewhere, that a picture, and, I believe, a natural landscape, has a shut-up, stifled look, unless there is water in it. I have felt that, I think; and now it seemed as if we were free again, with our fine prospect southward down the broad river. To the east of the camp was a grove of young trees, hung about with tassels of moss, and heavy cordage of strange vines; the trees just leaving forth under the influence of the Southern spring. In the edge of this grove, at the bottom - of a ravine, ran a little brook. From the trees we could gather moss and leaves to make our beds more soft, and in the brook we could bathe. Moreover, a few rods southward from the camp was a broad, deep bayou, approached by green, sloping banks, where we could swim as far and deep as we chose. It was luxury itself, Tuesday morning, to strip off our mouldy garments, and, while they lay sunning on the grass, wash the stiff muscles, and blistered, parboiled feet, in the brook, dappled darkly by the shadows of the boughs and leaves.

Our respite, however, was a short one. The night we arrived at this pleasant camp, the colonel passed down through the tents to see what our condition was. He stopped at Capt. Morton's tent, which was close by ours; and the captain brought out a bottle of currant wine, just from home, calling me up to have a sip also.

The colonel spoke very feelingly of the discomfort to which we had been exposed, and added, "At any rate, now we shall have a rest for a day or two." Tuesday forenoon, therefore, I paddled about in the brook at my leisure, feeling sure of ample time. At noon, however, the drum sounded once more; and the order came to pack every thing again, and fall in at once. Sudden orders had come, to march. This time, we were to go out to protect a heavy train of wagons, about to proceed out along the Port-Hudson road to gather the cotton stored everywhere in the planters' barns. Our march was along the same road we had previously traversed, and with similar incidents, though at first with less excitement; for it was no new thing now. The regiment was footsore, jaded, and suffering for the want of sleep. Both my collar-bones turned peace-democrats; and in every cell, with an ache for a tongue, protested against a further prosecution of hostilities. We toiled along, however; at every plantation, as we passed, seeing mule-teams loaded with cotton, and quantities of the snowy product tumbling from the windows and doors of sheds and barns.

We marched out seven or eight miles before we halted. As we advanced, we began to hear reports of the enemy from negroes; and at length reached a plantation from which a rebel force had just retreated. The rebels were hardly out of sight as we came up, and we followed close after them down the road. At length, within about five miles of the batteries, we came to a halt, and encamped in the edge of a grove, — for the night, as we supposed. Many of the men were much fatigued, and sadly footsore. The march had been a hard one for me; for the sun, during the afternoon, was most oppressive: but I made a cup of coffee, and cooked a dish of meat on my plate, and felt better. The men, generally, threw themselves on the ground at once, under the trees. Bivins, however, went to bathe in a brook near; and I took my seat to watch the baggage. It had just grown dark, when word was passed along the line, in a low tone, to be up and off at once.

It was hard enough; but it would have been the height of imprudence — two isolated brigades as we were — to spend the night within so short a distance of a powerful army of the enemy, perfectly aware of our being in the neighborhood. The grove, therefore, gave up its sleepers. In five minutes, the line was moving out of the shadow into the road, and, under the star-light, marching silently and rapidly back.

I like a night-march: the air is more bracing, the roads less dusty, and there is far more scope for ro-mance. In the afternoon, I had had a severe time; but the night-march home was an easy one. I could carry easily all my own baggage, though we were in heavy order; and occasionally spell the sergeant, who almost gave out with lameness, by shouldering the big flag. There was ample room for the play of fancy. The rebel scouts, no doubt, had already crept into the camp we had just abandoned, looking at the embers where we cooked our suppers to judge how long we had been gone; while the cavalry swept forward to occupy the road as we retired. The regiment, in general, however, suffered sadly. Many marched with bare, bleeding feet, and, toward the end of the route, sank to the ground with fainting limbs, to pass the night by the roadside. We reached our camp of the morning at midnight, — the colonel straight on his horse, sitting up in the starlight, at the entrance, to direct the column; his voice, as he gave the last orders, full of sympathy with his way-worn command. We only had strength to spread our rubber-blankets, and fling ourselves upon the ground.

Next morning, the regiment were a poor, languid crowd of hobbling cripples, — putting up shelter-tents with stiffened bones, crawling around fires to cook coffee, and fry, on their tin plates, pillaged meat and potatoes.

During the whole forenoon, those who gave out the night before came straggling in. This chronicler was tired and stiff; but he made out to wash his shirt and himself, — two undertakings requiring some degree of resolution. At night, however, I own, I was used up. I felt feverish, and next morning dosed strongly with quinine, which put Niagara Falls into each ear. During that day, I was on the sick-list. The next day, the regiment was ordered back to Baton Rouge. With some mortification, I left the regiment to march; and, with several scores of used-up men, made the passage down on a steamer.

I write now in the old camp, under the magnolias (which has become home to us), ragged, dirty, contented, burnt like an Indian, unkempt, unshaven, but about ready now for another start. During the week, we have marched fifty miles, heavily weighted, through mud, dust, heat, and a deluge of rain. We were on the brink of an engagement, having driven the enemy into the Port-Hudson intrenchments, — following them to within easy rifle-range of the batteries. We find it was not the intention of the general to fight a battle, unless himself attacked. We simply made a demonstration in aid of the fleet, a portion of which succeeded in passing up the river.

CHAPTER VIII.

THE GARDEN OF LOUISIANA.

MARCH 29. — This forenoon, we are encamped at Donaldsonville, — a point fifty or sixty miles below Baton Rouge, on the western bank of the great river. It is the pleasantest camp we have ever had. The neighborhood of this town, and the country along the bayou La Fourche, which here opens out of the Mississippi, is said to be the garden of Louisiana.

The landscape just about the camp here must be very like Holland. The tents are pitched in a perfectly level field, — stretching, without a fence, far and wide, with only here and there a tree. Along one side of the field runs the bayou, behind its Levee. The water now brims up nearly to the edge of this Levee, though on the land side there must be a slope of six or eight feet from the top of the bank to the surface of the land. If an opening were made in the Levee, our camp would be instantly drowned by the rush of waters. Sloops and schooners of considerable tonnage sail up and down the bayou, and one full-sized clipper-ship lies at anchor just opposite us. To see these craft, we are obliged to look up. The water-line of the bayou is about on a level with our eyes; so that the hulls and rigging of the vessels are in the air, over our heads. At the mouth of the bayou is a fort, with pointed angles, smoothly cut, and turfed with green. It is very regularly built, with ditch, counterscarp, bastion, and berme. This again, I imagine, is a feature which this landscape has in common with that of the Low Countries. Vauban himself might have built this little fort; and Marlborough and Villars would feel quite at home manœuvring here.

Of course, we have very little idea where we are going, or what we are to encounter; for we are the soldiers of a general who keeps his own counsel. In a day or two, we expect to march from here to Thibodeaux, and thence onward to Berwick Bay. We have left Baton Rouge, probably not to see it again during our term of service. We marched in the moonlight aboard the transport that was to bring us here, two or three nights ago. I lay on the upper deck, propped up by my knapsack, and took my farewell of the buildings on the Levee. I have taken my farewell of Ed.'s grave. I have done my best for it. The cross stands firm and straight at the head: the mound above it is high and smooth, and green with clover. The vine above, now full of blossoms, has snowed down upon the turf a whole deep drift of white petals; and sweet baby-buds, cradled among the whispering leaves and sprays, rock to and fro over it constantly in the wind of spring.

March 31. — At Assumpçion (I guess at the spelling). Charming, — perfectly charming, — day, place, sensations. We have marched twelve or thirteen miles since nine o'clock this morning, through the sweetest of regions, with the sweetest of air. Now we pause for the night, — the landscape still the mild, verdant, level expanse which made me think of Holland at Donaldsonville, — the grand bayou, deep and swift, riding along above the heads of the people. Here and there, the current, eating into the bank, leaves only a mere spadeful between the rush of the stream and the plain below it. The army began its march this morning at half-past seven. Punctually at the time, we had cooked and eaten breakfast. Our knapsacks were to go in baggage-wagons, — we carrying only blankets, equipments, and weapons. Among our indispensables, however, a few of us carry certain new arrangements. At McGill's suggestion, we have bought a coffee-pot, a frying-pan, and a kettle for boiling. Wivers carries the coffee-pot slung at his side : Sergeant Bivins carries the frying-pan strapped on his back, — handy, rather ; for when the excellent sergeant, at a halt, under the hot noon, shall throw himself backward on the sod. as soldiers do, he shall broil himself in an appropriate dish. I have, strapped to my belt, the boiler ; its crocky bottom painting thunder-clouds on the blue of my right thigh, as it swings to and fro. It will hold two or three quarts, and is up to flour. meal. eggs, oysters, or any thing which shall come to the omniverous haversack of the campaigner.

We have been brigaded anew ; being still in the second brigade of Grover's division, but with the Twelfth

Maine associated with us, instead of the Ninety-first New York. Col. Kimball, of the Twelfth Maine, is now our brigadier.

The conditions for marching to-day are excellent. Never did foot of military patriot press the broad sole of Uncle Sam's army-shoe into road at once so softly yielding, yet so firmly resisting ; and, for air, certain it is, that through scores and scores of leagues, in States openly or secretly secesh, — Mississippi, Tennessee, Kentucky, — certain it is, that over all this distance, this 31st of March, a *levée* of atmosphere of equatorial fervor had been built up. But, lo ! the currents of northern air broke through it in a perfect *crevasse* of coolness, inundating all these Louisiana lowlands with its refreshing tide ; so that, although we marched fast, the drops of sweat were beaten back, and the locks of the soldier, not plastered to his forehead, danced in a jolly manner in the breeze of home.

I have seen this day what I have not seen before, — estates which come up to what I have imagined about the homes of princely planters, two or three of them. The first we came upon was on the opposite side of the bayou. I was marching, not in the road, but along the ridge of the Levee, whence I could overlook the long column, the sugar-fields, and the distant wood, — a wood as romantic in its dim blueness as if I looked at it, not through a league or so of *space*, but through *time*, and beheld the Forest of Ardennes or the Grove of Cicero by the Fibrenus. While thus marching, — the bayou a foot or two from my path on one side, the road six or eight feet down on the other. — I caught sight of thick shrubbery, a chenille embroidery of green tufting the bare level plain. Then came into view a towering roof, and the stately palings of an enclosure befitting a princely domain. As we came opposite, down a long avenue, the perspective led the eye within the open portal of a splendid mansion ; from whose hall, ladies and children looked across at the marching army. Meantime, the air was full of sweet scents : for tropic plants, like Eastern princes, stretched forth their arms from the enclosure, and with odorous gifts flattered the passers-by ; and a tree full of bell-shaped blossoms — the airy "campanile" of the garden showing rows on rows of little purple chimes — "tolled incense" to us. One or two domains like this I saw, and many more less splendid, yet which were neat and pretty

Toward noon, it grew hotter again. The "crevasse" by which the north wind flowed in upon us was stopped up, and the hot, unfriendly air of the South had its own way with us. We were in light marching order ; but the burden bore heavily down. I remembered how Don Fulano talked to John Brent on the ride to deliver Ellen Clitheroe.

"Courage, noble master ! You ride me hard ; but I have a great reservoir of strength here in my loins and limbs. Never fear, you can draw on me without danger."

Something like that. I bestrode a more humble beast : "Shanks's horse" we used to call it, when we were boys. He made no such fine speeches. In fact, sometimes I feared he might give it up; but somehow the sinews and fibres always had a little more try in them.

The bands of the division are playing now at "tattoo." They have been playing during the evening with great vigor, particularly one bass-drum. The drummer, I believe, had to fall out to-day, on account of his ponderous instrument; and to-night is wreaking vengeance upon it, until it bellows through the camps far and wide. Bivins, who sits just the other side of the candle from me, believes "the boys are killing pigs, and have hired the bands to play to drown the squealing."

April 3. — We are in camp this morning, about three miles south of Thibodeaux, at Terre Bonne, which we reached yesterday afternoon. The railroad from New Orleans to Brashear City is a few rods north of us, — a road which our forces hold, and along which, this forenoon some time, when the engines can get to it, the second brigade expects to take its first car-ride in Louisiana.

We shall carry home a much more favorable impression as to the resources and civilization of this State than we should have had if we had not passed through this country of the La Fourche. From Donaldsonville to Terre Bonne, a distance of nearly forty miles, the aspect of the country varies but little. It is thickly peopled; the plantations succeeding one another as do the farms in any populous agricultural region of the North.

Seldom does an army march under circumstances so delightful. The miles were not weary ones; for the same really remarkable conditions made our progress comparatively easy from first to last, — a bright sky and sun, but a cool northern breeze, and a road, for the most part, in perfect condition to receive the soldier's foot-fall. On one side rose the slope of the Levee; ten or twelve feet high from the road, two or three from the water on the other side. When the column halted, we could run up the slope, then stoop to the cool bayou to drink, or to wash face, hands, and feet. On our right, as we marched, we passed, now houses of moderate size, bare of elegance — sometimes even squalid in appearance; now, again, mansions of comfortable look; and, not unfrequently, beautiful seats, set up high to preserve them from danger in case of a crevasse, with colonnades ornamented tastefully with orange-groves and the glorious live-oak, with *trees* full of roses instead of bushes.

Plantation after plantation! Along the road were white palings, or often the pleasanter enclosure of a rose-tree hedge, with white roses all out, and the green of a richer depth than we know it. Sometimes the planter and his family looked out at us from behind a " protection " posted before them on the gate, seated upon the broad portico under the wide roof, beneath wide-spreading awnings, with open doors and windows behind. Then, between house and hedge, these marvellous gardens! Tall trees overhung them; with vines, sometimes nearly as thick as the trunks, twining,

supple as serpents, from root to topmost bough, —
twining, hanging in loops, knotted into coils.   Then,
underneath, flowers white and delicate, adorned with
dewy jewels, scented with odors incomparable; flowers
uncouth and spiny; the cactus, not here exotic, but " to
the manor born," its gnarled and prickly stem thickly set
with purple buds.   The air would be pungent with
sweetness as the column marched past.

Such tropic luxury of air and vegetation !   These
scents and zephyrs; the bird-songs we heard; the
summer-blue of the heavens; the broad palm-leaves at
the planter's portico; these blossoms of crimson and
saffron and white; this slow-moving air, so burdened,.
and laboring under its freights of perfume, — all these
are such as Paul and Virginia knew; all these, and I
suppose, too, the foil to all these, — the miasma of the
swamp close at hand, and the poisonous serpent lurking
here.

When the garden was passed, generally we came to a
huge gate, upon and about which would be clustered
the negro force of the whole estate, old and young.
From this a road ran, down which, at the distance of a
quarter of a mile perhaps, we could see the white
chimneys of the sugar-mill; the village of negro cabins;
then acres on acres of cane-field, stretching clear to the
heavy forest on the verge of the horizon.

At noon of yesterday, we came to Thibodeaux.   As
we entered the village, the drums struck up.   The
footsore men forgot to hobble; the melting men forgot
their heat.   We were all straight and soldierly; for the

march was nearly finished. The streets of the village were full of people, upon whom it became us to make an impression ; and the sound of the drum and fife is a spur to the soul. We were dusty and sweaty ; but I think we made a good appearance. The colonel was on his horse again ; the day before, and to-day, he had walked more than half the route, giving his horse to tired privates : so the chaplain, who has carried a gun and knapsack, besides going on foot. We unfurled the two flags, and set them upright. The road, as we approached Thibodeaux, had been growing even more lovely ; and now, in the village, the climax of beauty was reached.

To go from Baton Rouge to Thibodeaux is like changing from the outer petals to the heart of a full-blown rose. Baton Rouge, once fresh and pretty, is now curled up and withered by the heats of war ; but the blossom grows fresher, and here in the centre is the reservoir of honey, — the place where the bee sucks. Each little cottage had its garden ; every gable was embowered ; every window and pilaster buried in vines ; every garden gilt-edged with ripe oranges along the borders. Puffs of wind, like scented exquisites, sprang out over the blossoms, — the gayest sprites that ever were, — and, seizing for partners our two colors, — rather faded and dishevelled belles, — danced them up and down in a brisk measure. The streets of the village were full of its hybrid population. Very few jet-black ones there were, and not many thoroughly white, but throngs on throngs of mixed-blood, — from

deep mulattoes, up through quadroon and octoroon, to
fair boys and girls with complexion just made rich and
vivid with a dash of the tiger-lily. Not a pleasant or
creditable story is it, — this tale of corruptness which
we can read in the faces of the population whenever we
pass through a village, or scan a crowd of plantation-
hands gathered on a fence or under a hedge to look at
us as we pass.

April 5. — At the " Bayou Bœuf." The bayou is
one of those characteristic Louisiana water-courses
which do so differently from water in other parts of the
world, — riding over a district, instead of boring its way
through it. The land slopes back from the river-bank ;
so that the drainage of our camp is toward the swamp,
a short distance in the rear, instead of toward the
bayou. It is a dreamy afternoon. A heavy haze
buries the distance, and veils even the trees and plantations a little way off on the other side of the stream.
I sit on the huge root of a live-oak, whose heavy top
hangs far out over the water, giving me a dense shade, —
me and the brilliant little minnows that I see swimming
up in shoals in the quiet water, as I raise my eyes.

We did not leave Terre Bonne until yesterday forenoon ; making the whole time of our stay there a day
and a half. We were piled, thick as we could sit, upon
platform-cars, and then brought eighteen miles to this
point. The road was a level, broad-gauge track, over
which the engine drew us rapidly. We had the best
opportunity we have yet had of seeing a wild Louisiana
morass. For a long distance, we went through a dense

cypress-swamp, — such an one as we have not seen
before, — a dense growth of cypresses, with a very
heavy undergrowth between the tall trunks, and, beneath that, a thick mat of water-plants lying upon the
surface of the fen. It was like a wall of vegetation,
almost, on each side; through which, occasionally, we
could see deep, dark bayous flowing, and black pools.
Alligators several feet long lay on logs, or in the
water, with their backs just rising above; and, on
floating timbers and little islands of earth, snakes,
single or in coils, lay basking in the sun. Later in the
season, I suppose, we should have seen even larger
numbers of this agreeable population. Huge vines,
coiled into knots, bound the cypress-trunks and other
growths into one mass of vegetation. We saw, too,
numbers of palms; which here grow short, by stumps
and pools, spreading abroad their wide-divided leaves,
as if they were showing hands at cards.

April 10. — We have made another move, and are
now at "Brashear City," — on the embouchure of the
Atchafalaya, — a city which consists of a wharf and a
railroad-depot, and but little besides. My feet rest in
the crushed clover, upon which our blankets were
spread as we slept last night; and through the opening
of the tent, just far enough off to prevent our being
swept away by the tail of some enterprising alligator,
I see flowing the bayou, with sugar-houses on the
opposite shore, and cypresses behind, — the tall, dark
trees that tell of swamps.

We are close on the enemy again. A strong fort,

in their hands, is only seven miles distant; and yesterday afternoon we marched to the sound of distant firing from Weitzel's advanced corps. During the night, too, the air was pervaded with the sublime shiver and boom of distant cannonading. I sit in clover, for the time being: but every minute I expect the drum-call; for we are here only temporarily, in light order, and expecting rapid and severe movements.

We took up the line of march yesterday under circumstances which I have several times described, — brilliant enough, but becoming now an old story; though I own I am not so hardened that I was not thrilled to hear a fine, full band play, "The dearest spot on earth to me is home," followed by a regiment stepping strongly to the air. It proved to be, by all odds, our hardest march for me; although it was only about nine miles. The sun was bitterly hot, and the dust heavy. For the first time in my soldiering, with a red face and blistered feet, I was obliged to turn aside from the regiment, and stop under a tree to throw away part of my load. It was not, however, until men in whole sections had been wheeling up, and stopping by the roadside for a long time; so that I had a good part of the regiment for company in my first falling-out.

I have now seen numbers of streams and much country, and am familiar with the strange aspects of a Louisiana landscape. Of course, we know, that, on this globe, water plays the principal part, and land is secondary. As Northerners know nature, however, it is land that is most exulting, bounding, as it does,

6

into hills, standing kingly in mountains; while water, more humble, hides in glens, or flows in submissive rivers before the feet of lordly ranges. Here, however, water bears itself arrogantly, — floating sometimes above the level of the soil; sometimes just even with it, as here, where the ripples of the brimful stream threaten the clover-flowers, which are scarcely above them. Meanwhile, a furlong or so in the rear, is the swamp, as ever, close at hand, — the traitor in the heart, ready to help the foe outside. Water is thus haughty and encroaching; while land is a poor, cowed, second-fiddle-playing creature, — only existing, apparently, that water may have something to pour itself out over and exhibit itself upon.

Then, too, the painful sycophancy of the vegetable kingdom! It owes its whole existence and consequence to land, if any thing does; yet here, like a set of false-hearted flatterers, trees and weeds go toadying the ruling power. The forests are watery : old trunks robe themselves in moss, counterfeiting the appearance of discolored growths of coral; and, along the brinks of bayous, stout-hearted live-oaks even, that ought to be ashamed of themselves, bend almost horizontally over the currents, or indeed, sometimes, as in one case right here in our camp, hold on by the roots, and grow *downward* almost, letting the water flow around and over them, just raising their tops above the stream, a rod or two out from shore, — all this fawning and hanging-on, instead of growing straight up, and flinging out their tops like independent and self-respecting growths!

CHAPTER IX.

VICTORY.

APRIL 13. — Rather a stirring accompaniment to your scribbling pencil to have a furious cannonade going on within two or three miles, — to have fresh in your memory the sharp skirmish which took place on the very spot where you are seated, only a few hours ago; and all the time to have the Second Massachusetts Battery harnessed up in the road, with the men on the horses and seats; to know that when they whip up we shall be ordered in, and that our business will be to support this battery through thick and thin, — the thick, just at the present, being most probable. It is early in the afternoon. The hot sun beats down upon us, who have stacked our arms here in this shadeless cane-field, and seated ourselves among the furrows. Perhaps we shall have time to eat a hard tack and make a hasty cup of coffee before we start.

To-day is Monday. Saturday, we embarked at Brashear City, leaving a fine, airy, roomy camp for —

" Fall in ! "

April 14. — This day I have seen a bloody battle fought, and now write sitting among furrows cut up by the wheels of the batteries. A little way to the right, in the edge of the wood, lie the unburied dead. There, too, lie the castaway guns and all the wreck and waste of such a field. A few rods to the left, the surgeons, all this forenoon, have been dressing wounds. The pursuit of the enemy is going forward. We only wait the order to advance. Occasionally the strong, fresh south wind brings to us the crash of a volley, or an explosion in the advance. A huge vapory column builds itself up into the air; then the breeze dissipates the unsubstantial tower from base to cornice.

April 17. — I have to drop and catch my pencil as I can; for we are doing tremendous work. O people who clamor for rapid movements! if you only knew what forced marches after a flying enemy cost us poor fellows, who have to make them! — the burden being so heavy, the roads so dusty, and the noon-sun so burning hot. It is Saturday morning. Since Wednesday morning, we have pursued the flying rebels fifty miles. I have just seated myself, with my stiff limbs stretched on the grass, under the shadow of a rough stable belonging to a miserable plantation in these back regions of Louisiana. I only make this little note; for the pursuit is not ended, and I ought to use this respite for sleeping and eating rather than writing.

April 21. — As you see, during the past week or so, I have occasionally caught up my pencil among the most tremendous and unspeakable exertions, simply to record my whereabouts, and that I lived. We are in camp now at Opelousas, far toward Texas, in the back

regions of Louisiana ; having pursued the retreating enemy seventy-five miles. Remember, we have made this
distance on foot, under a heavy burthen. Thank God
with all my heart, I am perfectly well after the march,
though I have been fearfully tired, and once was at the
lowest point of exhaustion. We understand that we are
to rest here, and prepare for a still further advance ; but
our forced marching, I presume, is for the present
over.

I have now leisure to go back, and give the details of
this experience of hardship.

On Saturday, April 11, Grover's division embarked
at Brashear City Our brigade left a delightful camp
for the transport " St. Mary's," a beautiful vessel, but
one aboard which we underwent a packing, to which the
stowage aboard the " Illinois " was nothing, and which
certainly nothing could parallel but the packing of a
slaver. Our boat carried three regiments, the horses
and greater part of the men of a battery, and I know
not how many more. I only know I took my post on
a little rise in the deck, between the smoke-stack and
engine, built up to cover the machinery. I was there
with about ten others, and hardly left it from that Saturday night until near noon of Monday ; not because I
was shackled to the spot exactly, but because I could
hardly take a step without treading on some one. By
daytime, we sat with our legs curled under us, under a
blazing hot sun, under which we almost *popped* out on
the deck like kernels of corn on an iron plate. By
night, we tried to sleep, with the plunging piston with-

in reach of the hand. I lay with my head lower than my feet, my head on my knapsack, my feet passed up over the shoulders of Grider and another of our fellows, with Callighan's elbow in one side, and Bivins's head upon my breast. How dreary was Sunday! I awoke unrefreshed. There was water all about us, but none to be had for washing, and not much to drink. Toward noon, I managed to buy some fine oranges of a cabin-waiter, which helped my poor dinner of the hardest biscuit and coarsest salt beef. We were in a great strait for coffee, which, for a long time, seemed utterly out of the question. At length, however, Joe Pray, a "cute" genius, was inspired. Just in front of my place rose the escape-pipe of the steamer, ten or twelve feet above the deck: from this, hot steam was constantly issuing. Joe was seen to eye this, to grow thoughtful, then to pour a handful of ground coffee into his can-teen, partly filled with water. With this he came to the foot of the pipe; and, after a few efforts, he tossed the canteen clear over its edge into the current of steam, holding it by its long white string. It was an entire success. Joe withdrew in a few minutes with a canteen full of hot, well-steeped drink. As he squeezed his way back to his place, there was a crowd to profit by his experiment. The old pipe puffed away, and many were the coffee-makers who invoked blessings upon the head of Joe Pray

Night came again, and I slept as before, with men crowding everywhere; and, beneath me, four or five mus-kets not covered over   I got up in the morning tattooed like a Carib, where the steel projections of the muskets had pressed into my back and legs.

Meantime the sail was monotonous and uninteresting. We ploughed along, stirring into waves the sallow torpor of the bayou, — the low shores on either hand walled up with the massive vegetation of the climate. At length, we emerged into a broad lake, the " Grand Lake," environed by what seemed to us only wilderness. The grim, battered old gunboat that *bossed* the expedition went ahead with cannon run out, examining narrowly each point for masked batteries.

At last, it was Monday morning. When the fog lifted, a regiment or two were put ashore from the fleet, and found a body of rebels on hand to oppose the landing in a sharp skirmish. "Bang!" went a field-piece on shore, which brought us all to our feet. Then followed a roll of musketry ; then presently, with a heavier boom, the gunboat put in its 'word, — a puff of smoke ascending quickly from its rusty ports ; then the crash of the explosion, — a long whistle from the flying shell, — presently a jet of fire against the dark thickets on shore ; and, in a minute or two, the sound of the bursting coming faintly to us from afar. A planter's mansion, with sugar-house and negro-cabins, stood on the shore ; behind which buildings we could see columns of men in motion, under the white smoke of the skirmish, which now rose to the tall tree-tops. The grim gunboat, the " Clifton," guided by signal-flags on shore, sent out, now a solitary puff, now three or four nearly together ; while, in the pauses between these heavier firings, came from the shore the fainter fusillade, linking the peals into an uninterrupted concert. At length, it ceased. The enemy retired, and we had opportunity to land.

We marched back from the river into the cane-field, where I had time to write a line or two in my journal. A few regiments and batteries pushed ahead at once; but we remained long enough to have pailfuls of coffee made and passed from man to man, — delicious enough under the circumstances. Under the roof of the sugar-house, Gen. Grover walked to and fro with his hands behind him, and head bent forward in anxious thought. Two rebel prisoners were under guard close by; and, from the vessels, horses and stores were being landed in all haste. It was a critical moment. We had come upon the rebels unexpectedly, and the general meant to profit by the surprise. One of the transports, however, with a brigade aboard, which could not be spared, was hard aground a league back in the lake. After some delay, however, it was afloat again, and came up.

In the early afternoon, we were on the march. We plunged into a tall forest, where there was a dense undergrowth of canes; the under and upper growth striking hands together to keep the sun out, and have the road underneath a perpetual quagmire. The road was heavy, and cut deep with artillery-wheels, through whose ruts we waded and jumped, with every now and then the sound of cannon (to stimulate us) from the advance. To the wood, a broad open space succeeded, on which were drawn up the regiments thrown forward in the morning. Here signs of strife appeared, — two wounded cavalry-men; one hurt in the leg, the other more dangerously wounded, muffled in his blanket upon a stretcher. We could look forward now a mile or two; and, when the reports came back, could see beforehand the white smoke of the discharge. We thought we had come into a savage region, so wilderness-like had been the shores of the bayou and the lake; but, once through the belt of woods, we found ourselves in a smiling land again. Presently we struck the Têche, — here not more than fifty yards broad, — flowing between banks, that, for a delightful wonder, *sloped down* from higher land on each side to the surface of the stream, — banks, with clumps and groves of trees, with sugar-houses to be seen here and there in the distance, and handsome mansions.

We were passing on in the direction of the firing, which gradually advanced as we pushed forward; not so fast, however, as to prevent our gaining upon it. At length we crossed the Têche by a bridge which had its timbers charred in several places. The advance found it in flames, and just saved it. The embers were hardly cold. Companies of the Fifty-second now deployed as skirmishers. A section of the Second Massachusetts Battery went out across a field, under charge of a straight, finely riding lieutenant; and presently they were at it, throwing shells into clumps of trees where there were suspicious signs. The skirmishers opened out into a long line, with intervals of two or three yards between the men; then advanced cautiously toward the buildings and fences. As the colonel galloped by, —

6*

"I have one man wounded," said the captain of the company behind the colors. "A shot just grazed his arm."

We were close upon them, and came to a halt. It was nearly nightfall, and we could not advance in the darkness. Over the fence, in front of our line, twenty rods or so, was our line of skirmishers; and beyond them, in the gathering dusk, across the wide plain we strained our eyes to see the little moving spots, — the pickets of the enemy. A squad of rebel prisoners went by us, just taken, under convoy of cavalry. They were stout, well-fed men, — some in the butter-nut dress, some in gray. Their clothing looked serviceable, and was in as good condition as the clothing of soldiers is likely to be during a hard campaign.

Here is something even more interesting. A short distance behind us, we noticed a very handsome plantation and mansion, down the road from which comes now, in haste and in much agitation, a stately lady. She is a matron of fine bearing, elegantly attired. Her face is full of character; she is bareheaded; in age, perhaps forty-five or fifty, but with hair still jet-black and abundant. She sweeps by us hastily, with the majesty of a noble mother of Rome, and stops at the stirrup of Gen. Grover, who has halted at the cross-roads, just beyond where I am standing. She has come to intercede with the general for her son, who has just been taken prisoner, — a fine, fierce boy of nineteen or twenty, who stands, haughty and tall, close by, among a group of captive rebels.

"Do let him go, general: he is all I have!" (repeated again and again.)

Most earnest and stately intercession! But the boy has been taken in arms; and the general, I believe, refused to listen. The negroes say this matron owns two miles square of country here, and four hundred slaves.

We camp, as we often do, in a ploughed field. We are sadly in want of sleep; for, during the two previous nights, we have had almost none. We do not stop to pitch tents, but lie down on the furrows, trying to make provision against the impending rain. Down it comes at midnight, then at intervals until morning. Meantime, the wind blows fresh, and the rubber-blankets go flying off from us into the mud, leaving the water to pelt us as it chooses; another tough and almost sleepless night. Our equipments, of course, are all on, and our loaded guns at our sides, to guard against a night surprise. At four o'clock in the morning, wet and unrefreshed, we are on our feet again. There is no time for making coffee; we are ordered into line at once, and march forthwith into fearful scenes.

It appears now, that, when we landed from the transports, we were not many miles from a strong force of rebels posted near Franklin, which force Grover's division was to assail on the flank or rear. Banks, with the main body of the army, had advanced up the Têche toward the same point, had driven back the rebels in our direction, and now the two Union armies were about to effect a junction; not, however, without sacrifice.

Day broke, as we marched out into the road, — a listless, half-exhausted body of men. During the three previous nights we had had little sleep, and but little food since the Saturday before. It was now Tuesday. We were all more or less drenched with the rain, and the blankets and clothing weighed double with the moisture. As the sun came up, however, and the morning damps steamed off, we felt better, and had our senses open a little to the beauty of the road, the sweetness of the blossoms, and the verdure of the slopes.

Presently we hear the sound of firing.

"They have found them again," I say to the color-sergeant; and we look off over the woods to where the white cloud of the discharge can be seen rising among the trees. As we sweep along the road toward the firing, the day each minute becomes more and more beautiful. Each minute, too, the roar of cannon is more frequent, and becomes mingled at last with sharp, rattling volleys of small-arms.

We come, at last, into full view of the scene. We halt in the road; and leaning against a fence, looking southward through the rails, the whole combat is visible to us, who are now within cannon-range. We look down a gentle slope. To the left we can see a battery posted, which fires very vigorously; then bodies of infantry, in long, dark lines, moving upon an open field in front of a wood. In the lines are gaps, which may be caused by moving over rough ground, or by the plunge of shot and shell. To the right, again, we can see bodies of troops, and batteries. Hear that long crash of musketry ' each individual discharge so blending into the others, that we can only hear one long sound, like the slow fall of some huge tower. It is a rebel volley, terribly effective, as we afterward hear; and, while the wind bears it to us, we are ordered forward, and presently are on the very field.

Ambulance-men, with stretchers, are hurrying across the field to a sugar-house in the rear, where a hospital is established. On each stretcher is a wounded man, and the number of these makes it certain to us that the engagement has reached the sad dignity of a pitched battle. We are passing ammunition wagons now; now a tree, beneath which is a surgeon at work; and, close where he stands, on his back, stiff and stark, dead, a tall, broad-chested man, with closed eyes. The column files to the right, out of the road; and we stand in line of battle just in the rear of the action, within rifle-range of the woods where the enemy lie concealed, expecting every moment the order to advance. The firing, however, slackens; and presently word comes that the enemy are withdrawing.

Between the color-company and the next company, through the centre of our line, runs the cart-track down into the field, along which now is constantly passing a stream of wounded men, on stretchers, or supported by comrades, and lines of rebel prisoners. I am close by, and can hear the talk of a sergeant, bloody, but able to walk, who is glad he has had a chance to do some service. I look, too, upon the ghastly head of a young lieutenant, who is dying upon his stretcher, and upon many others. Prisoners come by in squads, — sometimes five or six, sometimes twenty or thirty ; some in gray, some in blue, some in faded brown. Once in a while, there is an intelligent, good-looking face ; more often the features are unintelligent, — the brutish face of that deteriorating class, the white trash. Thus we stand close at hand to suffering and death.

The pursuit is being continued down the road. Hours pass, and we still remain in line. We cook, eat, and sleep. I get out my portfolio, and write a little. In the course of the day, up into the blue, calm sky go mighty columns of smoke, with deep reports, — the explosions of rebel gunboats and transports, overtaken in the Têche by the victorious army, and blown up by their crews as they flee. Within half a dozen rods of our line is a field-hospital, where lie, of one New-York regiment, the wounded colonel, the dead lieutenant-colonel, adjutant, and other officers and men. Of other regiments, too, are many wounded, federal and rebel, — some dying under the surgeon's hands. I go over and see the writhing wounded, and the hospital attendants laying out the dead. An Irish private lies close by the straight young adjutant, whose face is reverently covered ; and not far off is a rebel, covered thick with his own gore. Before death go down all distinctions and animosities.

Does it not seem, when the experiences are so out of the common course and so dreadful, as if there ought to be some change in outward circumstances to make

them correspond? But no: it was a perfect summer
day, — an almost cloudless sky, with a cool, sweet wind
coming from the woods where the rebels had been hidden; the woods green and fresh and innocent, as if
they were only a haunt for fairies.

Toward night, I go down the cart-path to the actual
field, and see the broken muskets. the scattered knapsacks and clothing, the furrows where the enemy lay,
the bloody pools where the dying fainted, the burial
parties, and the piles of distorted corpses lying by the
trenches just dug to receive them. I have wished, that,
so long as Ed. was to die, he might have met his death
in the front of battle, with a manly shout upon his lips,
and the light and ardors of the conflict shining forth
upon his face: but it is more dreadful than I had believed; and now I thank God that we could lay his fair
young body in the grave, undesecrated, — with the limbs
unbroken, with no gash upon his youthful brow, nor
gory stain upon his noble breast.

They say we lost in the neighborhood of four hundred. Only one brigade was engaged. It was a bloody
strife.

CHAPTER X.

PURSUIT.

As the shadows grew long, we were ordered into line again. I had just returned from the edge of the woods where the conflict had been severest, and the dead were being buried. I cast a farewell glance at the fence, along the rails of which the rebels had rested their pieces in the morning; at the dense trunks filled in with broad palms and thick standing canes that had been their cover; at the group burying the dead, a rebel prisoner standing at the elbow of the sergeant in charge, giving him the names of a pile of the enemy about to be interred; then we marched off. As we passed the sugar-house, amputations and other severe surgical operations were being performed. We went only a short distance, then encamped in a broad field sloping down to the Têche. Permission was given to get from the neighboring plantations what was needed in the way of food; and, after an exciting day, the regiment was soon at rest, — rest we had earned by the hardships of the three or four previous nights, and which was invaluable to us as we came to undergo the privations and labors of the following days.

The camp was early astir on Wednesday. We bathed in the Têche, and watched the " Clifton," our old, grim friend, which came steaming up; the coast being now clear for her through the explosions of the day before. As soon as she had passed, it was time for us to go; for word spread that the rebels were retreating into the interior, that we were to follow them at once, and that this gunboat in the bayou, which generally flows near the road, was to guard the flank of the pursuing column.

The march was most fatiguing; though in a proper conveyance, that glorious day, the road would have been very fine. Through some mistake, we had retained our knapsacks, and so were in heavy order, although the army in general only carried the lightest possible load. We passed the mansion of the stately lady who pleaded for her son, where, a few days before, it was said, the Confederate generals had been entertained at a splendid ball. The road here was bordered by a hedge of orange-trees, whose fruit the soldiers could pick as they passed. We saw signs everywhere along the road of great wealth. The country of the Têche, like that of the La Fourche, is a garden region; fine plantations succeeding each other continually; the sugar-houses looming large back on the estates; the negroes gathering upon the fences and gates by the roadside, of all shades, of all degrees of ugliness and beauty. Sometimes a hedge bordered the road, — of heavy, opulent foliage; sometimes rich fields spread away beyond the fences; sometimes the bayou opened a few rods away, the current flowing between the sloping oak-dotted banks. When the bayou was concealed, we could often hear the regular clank of the "Clifton's" machinery, steadily keeping pace with us, as we plunged deeper and deeper into the heart of Rebeldom.

We came to a spot where the negroes say the rebels meant to make a stand, — then thought better of it. We imagined the sallow, haggard hosts waiting in their butternut-coats behind the fences; then panting forward again, as the hoof-beats of the Federal cavalry came within hearing. The day grew burning hot. We marched rapidly on, stopping occasionally to catch our breath. Under every tree lay a group of panting men. It was a forced march. Gen. Banks knows every commander has been censured for not following up successes; and now the successes were to be followed up. Right that it should be so! Honor to our leader's energy! But, you people who clamor for rapid movements, how little do you know what these things cost the poor infantry-soldier! This day I felt well, and marched with the best; though, when it grew to be late afternoon, there was something cruel about the steadfastness with which the blue-and-white brigade-flag kept the road in advance. It was long before we saw it waver, then turn into a field to the right, where was to be our bivouac. We accomplished, that day, twenty-five miles, by universal agreement; marching from seven in the morning until near sunset, with an occasional rest of from two to fifteen minutes.

The trouble is, that, when the halt comes, you cannot begin your rest for a long time. First, wood must be got. The load must be unslung from the back and waist; then, no matter how weary you may be, your only chance is to run at full speed, with the rest, to the fence designated to be used for fuel. Then there is a tug for that; in which your temper must be *chained* to you, if it is not lost. Then the tent must be pitched; fresh water got; rations drawn; supper cooked; and perhaps, as happened to me this day, you have to sit up till midnight to get the company's share of the beef that is being killed during the evening.

During the night, the enemy fled again; and early in the morning we were in pursuit. The road was still beautiful; the plantations, as before, rich with sugar-houses, gardens, and well-filled poultry-yards, which stragglers and negroes, who follow the army in hundreds, made free with. The heat became most oppressive. I have never found marching so difficult. Men, by platoons almost, exhausted by the rapid walk of the regiment, were turning in under hedge and bush. Some, too, not exhausted, put on the pretence of it, and fell behind, only to have opportunity to pillage when the army had passed. I was determined to stand it while I could: but hotter grew the sun; the dust filled the stifling air; the rests seemed infrequent. I was at the last point of exhaustion. I turned aside under a clump of bushes, and had just time to fling open my belts and straps, when my brain swam. I reeled, and had just consciousness enough to direct my fall so as to have my knapsack for a pillow; then down I went,

— every pore a fountain, — completely used up.   I lay
in a stupor thus, — half conscious, half fainting by the
roadside, in the shade, — while within a few feet rolled
and rumbled onward the advancing and victorious army.
Now the tramp of infantry ; now the sound of battery-
wheels ; now the white-covered wagons.   "Yah moole !"
— I heard the darkey-drivers say to their mules, — "I
knows you's tired an' weak."   But there was no rest for
man or beast.   On they went, while I, lying there, half
gave my mind to the passing host, half dreamt of sweet
places, — home, and my cool, quiet study, far away.

Oh ! well, it was soon over ; and one ought to be
willing to march, even till he faints, to make a victory
gained in this cause more decisive.   At length, mem-
bers of the regiment began to come up, — farmers and
farmers' boys.   These sat down in my nook to "vow"
and "vum" and "van," in the most solemn manner,
that no hay-field or harvest experience ever came near
this.   So we rested.   A negro came by with chickens
and ducks slung on a pole.   I got a duck from him ;
then, from another, I got a handful of onions to flavor
the stew.   Then we went leisurely forward, and soon
were in the pleasant street of New Iberia ; by the side
of which, opposite a stately mansion, we found the
regiment again.

Not far from here is a salt-mine ; and a portion of
our brigade was detached at once, and sent to destroy
the works.   Meantime, we picked my duck, under the
thick shade that bordered the Têche ; then bathed in
the dark, smooth stream, among the empty whiskey-

barrels, which the rebels, only a few hours before, had staved by the score, and emptied into the water.

We supposed we were to halt for a day or two in this pretty village; but the enemy fled fast: so the next morning, early, we set out on another tedious march, — the order to " fall in " coming so suddenly, that we had no time to make coffee or take any breakfast. The drums beat as we went with conquering flags down the village street, — past the few rich mansions; past the Union Hospital (for we leave a hospital full of sick and worn-out men wherever we stop); past the hospital the rebels left behind them, with a pink flag at the gate; past Capt. Morton and the four companies of the Fifty-second, which we left behind as provost-guard. Soon we were beyond the village; and, after a mile or two, came to a turn in the road, where the advance, a little while before, had had a sharp skirmish. Six or seven dead horses lay in the road : one poor fellow, in butternut, lay stretched on the sod, — the morning light, bright and unpitying, on his dead, uncovered face. Five or six more were in a gully close by. There had been no time yet to bury them. We, the living, had not even time to eat; and were sweeping onward, without food, in our pursuit. We halted a few moments in front of a plantation. Toussaint, a monkey-faced negro attached to Company D, came out with a basket full of elegant tapers; and soldiers, who left the ranks to fill their canteens, brought out word of the splendor of the furniture, and the pillage it had undergone.

The character of the country changed soon after. We found no longer rich plantations, but came into a region broad and prairie-like, where, on the far-stretching plains, were feeding vast herds of cattle. The broad pastures of Texas, now, were not very remote; and this region must resemble the land of the ranch and lasso. The habitations became fewer, and of a much poorer character. We had no longer the bayou to run to for water; and could only fill our canteens at stagnant slimy pools, or stand and fight, at the few wells we came to, by the half-hour, for a drink, while the army hurried on. It was dreadfully tedious and hot. We marched, by the hour together, over the flat, dusty plains, under the burning sun. How intolerable it was! It was noon; but we were still without breakfast. The cartridge-box on one side, and haversack on the other, pulled very heavily; and gun and blankets doubled their weight.

It is now two o'clock, and we have sweltered and hobbled on some fourteen miles. I am sadly footsore at last; though, until now, I have had no trouble. I do not want to do myself permanent injury, nor bring on premature age and breaking-down; which I fear I shall do, if I make a regular thing of marching until I faint. "Mr. Grosvenor, will you fall out if I will?" Grosvenor is sick and weary, — not yet fully recovered from his fever in the winter, and only borne up by a most unconquerable spirit. He is more nearly spent than I am, and assents. We have half the regiment for company, strewn along the whole line of our march.

Pat O'Toole remarked the other night, referring to me, "Och! the cor-r-piral, shure, is tougher than a biled owl!" I shall lose such commendations in future, I fear.

Now that we have stopped, and left the dust and crowd of the column, the breeze blows cool. We lie and sleep under a little clump of trees for an hour or two, then make coffee in my boiler, — my dirty but invaluable utensil. I happen to have part of a fine chicken and some raw salt pork in my haversack. We find some onions in a garden near. At a poor house, close by, we fill our canteens at a well, among a struggling crowd of worn-out soldiers. The master, poor man! has lost almost every thing. We pity him and his little children, — all they have a prey to this thirsting and hungry soldiery. Grosvenor and I build our fire by ourselves, and presently we have a delicious soup bubbling. Grosvenor has salt and pepper; and, at the end of the afternoon, we have a grand dinner, steaming hot, — the first meal we have eaten during the day.

Sunset is not far off when we finish. We are now in better condition to move again, after our meal and sleep, though Grosvenor is really too sick and weak to stir. Two men, of a Maine regiment, come by with a handcart they have "confiscated." We get permission to throw in our burdens, if we will help draw the cart. In this way we pull and push forward a mile or two, our blistered feet making us limp at every step. Then we come to a wide plain, where the road is swallowed up; and every trace of the army disappears. I am for pushing on during the twilight, which is now falling, though we run the risk of being lost; but Grosvenor is too ill. The Maine men are worn out; and the vote is, to stay until the next morning in a deserted house used to store cotton. We spread the cotton on the floor for a bed. During the evening, other stragglers arrive, — Billy Wilson's men, Irishmen, negroes, — so that, by dark, the little house is full. One fellow has stolen a fiddle, on whose broken strings he manages to scrape out tunes. We listen to the fiddle a while, and wonder where the army is; but sleep comes very soon.

Next morning, we felt sure we had not far to go. We went two or three miles over the plain, guessing at the direction; and at length struck a road, along which it was plain an army had passed. Grosvenor fell by the roadside, too ill to go farther; while I set off to find water. I could find nothing but filthy pools of stagnant water, in which swine were wallowing, and into which bull-frogs large as chickens went floundering as I came up. The circumstances were forlorn enough for a sick man. At length, a train of battery-wagons passed. We "cheeked" it with a negro-driver, and jumped in over the tail-board of a forage-wagon, where we rode until we were ignominiously expelled by a sergeant. We had, however, reached the headquarters of Paine's brigade, Emory's division; and learned that Grover was just ahead, in the advance.

We managed to get hold of some beef and a spider, and cook a breakfast; Gen. Paine, in his spectacles, writing on the porch of a house close by. Then we tried to go forward again; but Grosvenor dropped after a few rods. I left him under a tree, and rushed back along the road to an approaching cart: "A sick sergeant; cannot walk; must join the regiment; will not take 'No' for an answer." So at last they took us both in. They were three soldiers of the One-hundred-and-fourteenth New-York, who had confiscated a good horse and a two-wheeled cart. They turned out to be good fellows; and now we got forward rapidly.

Gen. Banks and his staff went by us from the front. They all eyed us sharply, and we feared they had designs on our horse. The New-York men had had hard work to keep it out of the clutches of the cavalry; but this danger was passed like the previous ones. I watched the general's cool, resolute face, for signs of exultation. He had beaten the enemy in three battles; was driving them pell-mell before him, and possessing himself of a vast region of country full of wealth of every kind. I remembered Napier's description of Wellington after the battle of Salamanca, and looked to see a similar light on the countenance of our leader. He looked happy, certainly, and like a conqueror; though he was dirty and imbrowned, like the rest of us.

Soon after this, we halted in a grove, where were a large number of rebel prisoners under guard. Our companions cooked dinner, and I got out my portfolio. Sweat and rain had penetrated the pasteboard, and my little stock of paper was damp and discolored. I

7

managed to write a few legible lines. From here
was only about a mile to the camp of the regiment
which had marched eighteen miles the day before
They were in a grove, on the Bayou Vermilion. S
close were they the night before to the flying remnan
of the rebel column, that the bridge here was still i
flames, just becoming impassable. As they stacke
arms, a huge round shot came tossing in from the oppo
site bank, knocking down the guns, and causing a grea
scattering among the men. Of Company D, only fou
were left besides the captain, and Rogers, the first ser
geant ; the rest having all fallen out. Of the color
guard, none were left ; the adjutant getting off hi
horse, and bringing in the flags. Of the whole regi
ment which left Baton Rouge, about five hundre
strong, there were left that night, I think, only fifty
nine.

It was hard. Remember our packing aboard th
" St. Mary's," when rest was almost impossible, ou
exposure to the storm the night after we landed, an
then the marches. Our food was poor and insufficient
We were in what is called " heavy order." After th
early morning, the sun became very hot ; and the tread
ing of the long columns soon beat the roads to dust
Wednesday, we accomplished twenty-five miles ; Thurs
day, twelve or thirteen ; Friday, without an opportu
nity to cook any thing, eighteen or nineteen.

There was more to be done, however.

" Which is best," said the colonel, — " to undergo a
this fatigue and labor, or to fight bloody battles, an

lose half the regiment, besides giving the enemy time to prepare everywhere for our coming?"

Banks had the alternative to follow by forced marches on the very heels of the rebels, or to fight battles. If we had gone more slowly, they would have stopped and fortified, and been prepared to fight us again and again. Saturday night, the bridge was rebuilt. The Fifty-second was ordered across in advance of every thing, to guard it. We lay down after dark on the opposite bank, and presently were drenched by torrents of rain in a furious tempest. We lay in the pools, under the storm, until morning; then, with all our baggage weighing double, we started off through deep mud for Opelousas; accomplishing the march of about twenty-five miles during Sunday and Monday. Have we not earned our present rest?

I have just had a glance at a map. How little one can tell! Louisiana is done up neatly in pink. There is a cool-looking sheet of water, — that dismal grand lake, where we came so near "going up," all of us, aboard the "St. Mary's." From Franklin to New Iberia is a little stretch-up through the pink. How small! with not a hint of those choking, dusty leagues, along which we almost left our lives as we limped over them. Nor toward Opelousas is there any suggestion of those parched and dreary plains. It is unsatisfactory; but catch us forgetting what ache and sweat and hunger that distance cost us!

CHAPTER XI.

ON THE BAYOU COURTABLEAU.

APRIL 29. — This is the Bayou Courtableau, — a spot called Barre's Landing, about eight miles from Opelousas, whence we marched last Sunday. We are glad of the change. Water could only be got at our Opelousas camp by going a respectable pedestrian journey. Moreover, at our first coming, creatures by the score fell victims to our hunger. Parts of the carcasses of these had been left, and were tainting the whole neighborhood. We were not sorry, therefore, when the order came to march here, — a march we accomplished in a leisurely fashion, taking most of the day for it; mourning, some of us, that the day must go by without observance, like so many previous Sundays: but, on the whole, not an unhappy company; for we were rested now; and a night or two before, at dress-parade, we had heard Gen. Banks's congratulatory order, which told us we had done something, — taken a large number of prisoners, beaten the enemy in three or four battles, destroyed several gun-boats and transports, &c.

Opelousas was a dreary little place, where we found vegetating a population of French Creoles, — old men,

women, and children. The younger men are probably
all in the rebel army. McGill and I, one day, got
leave to walk about the streets. McGill was brought
up in Canada, and his patois appeared to serve him as
well with these Creoles as if he were in Quebec. Pro-
fessions of loyalty were plenty enough; but we imagined
they talked in a different strain a morning or two before,
when the wreck of the rebel army came panting through,
and the Texans took horses to escape to their own
State.

My arrest was my most noteworthy adventure at
Opelousas. It was the fourth or fifth day of our stay
there. I was tired of lying with the lizards under the
shelter-tent: so, as Bivins and two of the corporals were
going off on a sugar expedition, I joined them. We
went to the "Swayze Place," where my companions
had been before. They had given such accounts of its
elegance as to arouse our interest. We made our way
through a forest (killing a rattlesnake in our course),
entered the plantation gate, passed through a rather
squalid purlieu of negro huts, then came to the mansion itself, — a one-story dwelling, with neat veranda
and some marks of taste, though house and surroundings lacked finish. The garden was a wreck; and
through this we passed without hinderance, by the open
door, into what had been elegantly furnished apart-
ments. One had been a library; and the floor was
strewn with a litter of valuable books. One had been
a dining-room, at one side of which stood a handsomely
carved sideboard. In the parlor was a rich piano, and

other furniture in keeping, — all overturned, scattered, and marred. We went into bedrooms, where were handsome canopied beds, and heavy furniture of rosewood. In one was a large mirror, in which I caught sight of a very swarthy and travel-stained warrior, whom I should never have recognized.

I hurried out with an uncomfortable feeling. The pillage and destruction were due in part to our soldiers, in part to the negroes. It was discreditable and painful. At the sugar-house was sugar going to waste. My companions took what they could carry in their blankets, and I took from the deserted garden a handful of onions, — articles really necessary, short of rations as we were, and which we had been instructed we might take. Then we washed and filled our canteens from the broken bucket of the old well; then going forward, on our way back we met a company of men coming through the gate.

"Is it a picket, or what?" said we unsuspectingly; but, as they came up, they wheeled around us.

"Fall in as prisoners!" said the lieutenant in charge; and in we were forced to go, my companions with their sugar, and I with my fragrant burden.

First they marched us back, while they picked up cavalry-men and others prowling about as we had been. Then, with the arrested culprits, the guard set off through the woods for the camp.

We learned, in one way and another, that grave misdemeanors had been committed on the estate; that complaint had been made to Gen. Grover, and that the guard had been despatched at once to arrest all they could find. We passed the brigade in ignominious procession. What was to become of me? Word had gone back to my excellent parishioners at the North once before, that their minister and his comrades, when likely to go into danger, fortified their courage with doses of gunpowder and rum! Now he was arrested as a "merooder." Would it not be the last of me?

We reached the general's tent at last; the general, as is his habit, pacing thoughtfully up and down in front of it. "File right, file left; halt!" We are in the presence. One of the culprits was very *distingué* in a white shirt, — a "clean biled shirt," in campaigning parlance. This, it seems, he had stolen.

"Tie the man that stole the shirt to the fence here. Take the others to your camp, and keep them without food or drink until further orders."

On his heel again swings the general. "Right about, and forward!" to us.

In a dismal field we are left, with our feet in a ditch; the sun pouring down, and no shade. A bayonet, with a full-blown Paddy to manage it, blocks every avenue of escape. Toye and Stowell are hungry and wrathy; I am rueful; but Bivins makes light of his misfortunes. If the sergeant knew the words, I am sure he would repeat, "Stone-walls do not a prison make." As it is, he sports with his chains, and, so to speak, makes his dungeon ring with derisive laughter. We are in our shirt-sleeves, and dread the cold as night approaches. Toward dusk, I catch sight of a friend, just within hail, who is summoned with loud shoutings, and sent off with a message to the colonel. In about an hour, enter the colonel, on horseback, into the circle of firelight where we are sitting.

" Well, well ! how is this ? "

We tell him our story. We are ignorant of having broken any regulation. We are confined without judge or jury.

" Cannot you get us out? We want our hard tack; we want to go to bed."

The colonel has made strong representations to the general, to no purpose.

" Culprits are generally the most moral and orderly men in a regiment, according to their officers' showing. At any rate, your men were in very bad company, and must stand it."

All the colonel, even, can do, is to pass sympathy, as it were, through our dungeon-grate, and order over our blankets from the camp.

My friend who carried the message comes up again, when it is dark enough, and tips me the wink ; and, while we engage apparently in indifferent conversation (to delude the vigilant guard), a cold chicken is slipped from his blouse under my vest, and a pile of hard bread secreted under the blanket. In this transaction, however, we are detected by Corporal Billy Mulligan, the amiable functionary in charge. He, however, stooping, whispers, —

" Only kape thim from the liftinant, an' niver a word'll I say."

So we have a comfortable supper, in spite of Gen. Grover; then stretch ourselves across a furrow in the starlight. Morning does not bring us release, nor yet noon. Corporal Mulligan prophesies disgrace. Alluding to our badges as sergeants and corporals, it is, —

"Och, bys! but they'll be afther takin' thim stripes aff ye."

In the afternoon, we rig up a little canopy to keep off the sun. A grand review takes place. The Fifty-second marches by, little Claypole carrying the flag; Company D looking across the field to see their captured comrades. We wave our coats and caps, like men wrecked on a desert island to a passing ship. Grosvenor has got well, and waves back to us; so the others. At sundown, however, deliverance comes. Corporal Mulligan bids us an affectionate adieu.

"Be gorra! it's not mesilf that wanted to hould ye."

Gen. Grover vouchsafes no explanation of arrest or release. The dungeon yawns, and the oppressed go free.

Officers and men enjoy getting off sly jokes at me about my scrape; but, on the whole, I look back upon it with pleasure, as helping to round the cycle of my military experiences.

May 2. — We begin to see the wisdom of our rapid marching. We not only prevented the enemy from making a stand and fortifying, but we completely demoralized and dissipated his force, taking a large part prisoners. This chain of narrow bayous too, and shallow lakes, which we must hold unobstructed for navigation, if the country is to be held, could never have been gained but by our hasty marches. A night's intelligent work, by a few score of men, would put obstacles in the channels, which could not be removed for a long time ; but, so rapid and overwhelming was our rush, there was no time to accomplish even this. Then, too, there was no time for the destruction of property ; so that steamers now can come from New Orleans and Brashear City to this remote landing, bringing supplies to the army, and go back loaded to the water's edge with cotton and sugar. These products are found in great quantities, stored everywhere. A mountain of bales is piled up on the river-bank, to which hundreds of teams are continually adding. We are stationed here, with two or three other regiments, to serve as a guard while this property is being gathered. Is this hard? It is the Government policy, and would be thus defended. The owners of all this are rebels, who have fled at our approach, not waiting to take the oath of allegiance. It is right, therefore, to confiscate their property. It is a hard thing ; but it seems much less hard when you think that the wealth thus taken was accumulated by the unrequited labor of negroes. I remember the axiom at the foundation of the science of political economy, — that the basis of wealth is human work and sweat. Who should enjoy the benefits of the wealth, but those who work and sweat? It is right to take this, and use it in defraying our expenses in this war ; for in our triumph is coming the time of jubilee to these unpaid blacks.

Great barbarities, however, I fear have been committed. They say ear-rings have been torn from the ears of women, and brooches from their bosoms, while they sat with children in their arms. At Opelousas, an order of Gen. Banks was read, speaking of the conduct of the stragglers as bringing the deepest disgrace upon us, — disgrace so deep as almost to cancel the glory of the success. Of these enormities, I myself have seen 'but little. They were committed by stragglers; and except on one occasion, when I remained to take care of Sergeant Grosvenor, I did not spend a night away from my place in the regiment.

I have spoken of the fine mansion just this side of New Iberia, out of which Toussaint brought the handsome tapers. I did not go in; but men came out telling of the smashing of mirrors and furniture, and other ruthless vandalism. The destruction upon the Swayze Estate I saw after it was accomplished. I am glad that our regiment cannot be held guilty of any thing of this sort. There is a public sentiment among us which reprobates such acts. There are a few in each company, perhaps, who might take advantage of an opportunity, and be savages; but they do not represent us. Any thing necessary to our support we *did* take, and with the permission of our leaders. The wagon-trains were often far behind: we could not carry much in our haversacks; and, at any rate, coffee, hard bread, and salt pork, were pretty much the only food furnished. To support our exertions, we needed more abundant and palatable food. We made free, therefore, with herds, hen-coops, and plantation-stores, which were going to waste. Let me own up frankly to pillaging, — to having stolen onions in the Swayze Garden; to having assisted in the robbing of sugar-casks; to having held the candle while a lot of purloined cattle were being butchered. All this, however, I claim, was unavoidable; and it was certainly permitted. For the other unnecessary robbery, I disdain, for the Fifty-second Massachusetts, all connection with it. It is bad enough; but I believe it is foolish to call it unparalleled; as some do call it. I have read enough of war and siege, — of Magdeburg, of Badajos, of San Sebastian and Crimean outrages, — to know that such things are only the usual accompaniments of a great struggle. But how dreadful is war! how inexcusable, except when it is the only way to maintain goodness and refinement and truth against aggressive barbarism!

Our camp now is beautiful. Who is it (one of the Brontes?) who is so eloquent about her love for midsummer, with its white, opulent cloud-masses and superb verdure? This is the weather we have. Glorious heavens, and a glorious earth in forest and plain! and all night long the moon walks in splendor, transfiguring the soldier's brown face as he lies with his tent open to the wind, and his burnished weapons at his hand.

May 14. — A gentle rain is pattering on the tent-roof, — grateful to us now as a shower in August in Northern city or hamlet. To its soothing music the other men have gone to sleep; while I sit here with my back to the tent-pole, writing words to this pretty pat-

tering tune. May is going; and we are, generally
speaking, as idle here as during the previous month
we were active. It is nearly three weeks since we
encamped on the Courtableau, — weeks of glorious
summer. Day and night, along the bayou, the mock-
ing-bird "shakes from his little throat whole floods of
delirious music;" and over the stream, from the boughs
of the big trees, hang the ladders of moss, — the Jacob's
ladders, on which "the angels, ascending, descending,
are the swift humming-birds." The distant forest line
is blue to the eye, and of impenetrable density. What
enchanter's incense is this sweet blue haze! lulling the
outer sense, stimulating the fancy; so that I sit under
our booth, my eyes upon the far-away woods, dreaming
of romance, — just now of the "wood of Broceliande,"
and Vivien charming Merlin with her spells "of woven
paces and of waving arms." O sweet "Idyls of the
King"! is there any poetry like you? It is all beautiful. But our sojourn here is inglorious. Instead of
being left behind to guard cotton, I would have preferred to march with Banks to the Red River: a cup
of fatigue and hardship it would have been, but gloriously dashed with excitement.

The pile of cotton is a mountain on the landing. All
day long, — every day for weeks, — teams have brought
it in, until it almost seems worth while to build here the
factories that are to work it up into fabric; but, since
Mahomet will not come to the mountain (to set on its
head the saying), the mountain is going to Mahomet.
Down it goes, piecemeal, through the bayou, on little

steamers padded out like lank belles, at every available place, into portentous embonpoint. They say our business here will be finished when the cotton is carried away: so we watch the slow decrease of the pile, hear the mocking-birds, wash lazily in the bayou in contempt of alligators, and live along.

Along the bank of the stream is an immense camp of negroes. They have come by thousands from the whole country round. Generally, their masters appear to have fled; and the negroes, harnessing up the mules, loading in their families together with their own and their masters' goods, have come crowding in to us. They come trustingly, rejoicing in their freedom. By night, until long past midnight sometimes, we can hear them shout, pray, and sing. Gen. Ullman has been here, and the able-bodied men are to become soldiers. The women and older men, and all not fit for military duty, are to go on to plantations taken by the Government or by loyal men. They are to receive wages, and be well cared for. No doubt, their condition will be distressing in many cases. For them, it is a most momentous period of transition, — a crisis which they can hardly pass without suffering; but it will be temporary, and a bright future lies before them.

The other day, on the bank of the bayou, I found a man, born, as he said, in New Jersey. He came South as steward of a ship, and was coolly sold by his captain into slavery at New Orleans. From there he became a plantation-hand, and for fifteen years had been in bondage.

Last week, there came shivering through to us from
Port Hudson, forty miles away, the boom of a mighty
bombardment. We heard them, Friday and Saturday, getting the range; then Saturday night, — it was
starlight, and all calm as an infant's sleep, — that night
we heard the roar of the real attack, — continuous
thunder from the far north-cast. We could tell the
sharp reports of the Parrotts, the heavier boom of
Dahlgren, the long-drawn crash of mortar. The
whole air listened; and the land trembled, as if it par-
took in the guilt of its inhabitants, and quailed beneath
the blasting and thunderous retribution that was falling.
We felt it, rather than heard it, all through the long
night, coming through desolate fen and over plain,
through wood and over stream; imparting tremor to
every foot in those dreary, intervening leagues, as if the
Genius of the conquering North were making the land
feel everywhere the indignant stamp of her resistless
heel!

So we live and listen and wait. I am reduced now
to about the last stage. My poor blouse grows rag-
geder. My boots, as boys say, are hungry in many
places. I have only one shirt; and that has shrunk
about the neck, until buttons and button-holes are irre-
trievably divorced, and cannot be forced to meet.
Washing-days, if I were anywhere else, I should have to
lie abed until the washer-woman brought home the shirt.
Now I cannot lie abed, for two reasons: first, I am
washer-woman myself; second, the bed is only bed at
night. By daytime, it is parlor-floor, divan, dining-

table, and library, and therefore taken up. I button up in my blouse, therefore; and can so fix myself, and so brass matters through, that you would hardly suspect, unless you looked sharp, what a whited sepulchre it was that stood before you. I have long been without a cup. Somebody stole mine long ago; and I, unfortunate for me, am deterred, by the relic of a moral scruple which still lingers in my breast, from stealing somebody else's in return. My plate is the original Camp-Miller tin plate, worn down now to the iron. I have leaned and lain and stood on it, until it looks as if it were in the habit of being used in the exhibitions of some strong man, who rolled it up and unrolled it to show the strength of his fingers. There is a big crack down the side; and, soup-days, there is a great rivalry between that crack and my mouth, — the point of strife being, which shall swallow most of the soup; the crack generally getting the best of it.

Rations pall now-a-days. The thought of soft bread is an oasis in the memory. Instead of that, our wearied molars know only hard-tack, and hard salt beef and pork. We pine for simple fruits and vegetables. The other day, however, I received a gift. An easy-conscienced friend of mine brought in a vast amount of provender from a foraging expedition, and bestowed upon me a superb turkey, — the biggest turkey I ever saw; probably the grandfather of his whole race. His neck and breast were decorated with a vast number of red and purple tassels and trimmings. He was very fat, moreover; so that he looked like an apoplectic sultan. I carried him home with toil and sweat; but what to do with him for the night! If he had been left outside, he would certainly have been stolen: so the only way was to make a bedfellow of him. Occasionally he woke up, and "gobbled;" and I feared all night long the peck of his bill and the impact of his spurs. In the morning, we immolated him with appropriate ceremonies. The chaplain's coal-hod, the best thing in camp to make a soup in, was in use; but I found a kettle, and presided over the preparation of an immense and savory stew, the memory whereof will ever steam up to me from the past with grateful sweetness.

In spite of hard fare, I appear to flourish. The other day, I thought I was afflicted with some strange and terrible disease. I was growing short-winded, and had a novel fulness about the waist, which tightened my vest-buttons. Yesterday, however, I was weighed, and found myself fourteen or fifteen pounds beyond my usual weight. I was short-winded only because I was pursy; and the protuberant stomach was simply adipose. My gait, too, I thought was affected. Alas! is it simply that I waddle?

CHAPTER XII.

IN THE HOSPITAL.

JUNE 1. — A fortnight ago to-day, having obtained the requisite permit; having washed off the stains which rough work had left, and drawn a new blouse, — with the chaplain and surgeon, I embarked on the Courtableau for Brashear City. We left the Fifty-second under marching orders for the same point, — a long, tedious, fatiguing piece of work. I felt a little uncomfortable, hearty as I was, at riding down at my ease, while sick men must march it; but the errand upon which I was bound, I felt to be of the first importance.

The little steamer was loaded almost to sinking with cotton, contrabands, and soldiers of the brigade too feeble to endure the march of one hundred and thirty miles. We had for pilot a smart negro, who told me about the Red-River raft and the former difficulties of the Atchafalaya; through which stream he claimed to have been the first man to navigate a steamboat. The Courtableau was narrow and winding; densely wooded on both sides; the channel often running close to the boughs: so that, all the way down the stream, upon the branches had caught shreds of cotton from the bales aboard the steamers, as people carried into captivity by the Indians, in old times, left pieces of their dress to mark a path for pursuing friends. Alligators were numerous as turtles in a Northern mill-pond in hot weather, sunning themselves on logs or slimy banks, or swimming in the stream, — scaly, ungainly objects! a race left over from the pre-Adamite world, which ought to have received its quietus with the pterodactyls; yet a race not out of place in the swamp-country of Louisiana, which seems at least one whole geologic age behind the rest of the world.

The Atchafalaya, which receives the Courtableau, is scarcely wider than its tributary. The current we found very swift, and the river sometimes almost doubled backward. My black friend in the pilot-house, however, with one hand on the wheel and the other on the engine-bell, was equal to every crisis. We passed into snaggy lakes at last; then into the Grand Lake, where we saw the landing, from which, about a month before, we had advanced toward Franklin. In due time, we reached Brashear City; whence, the next day, we took the train for New Orleans.

I bought a handsome slab of marble, and caused it to be suitably inscribed for Edward's grave; and, when it was done, I took passage on a Government-transport for Baton Rouge. We left Baton Rouge early in April, full of troops; but now, with the exception of a few pale convalescents and a negro regiment, the streets were as innocent of drum-music and soldiers' tramp as if peace had come. The works near the cemetery had been built, during our absence, into a formidable citadel, frowning upon the eastern woods, and upon the river to the west, with mailed and weaponed brows. The grave, however, was unchanged; the cross, white at the head; the vine covering it deep, and still bearing a few late blossoms. I reared the marble in the early morning sunlight, to stand a pure and enduring sentinel until we can bring his ashes to rest nearer home.

At Baton Rouge, we heard first of the sudden investment of Port Hudson by Gen. Banks; and that every day, in front of the beleaguered fortress, such a battle was threatened as the department had never known. The transports were all detained to wait for this struggle; and even the sick had been sent up from the hospitals to do duty with the ambulances. There would be no opportunity to rejoin the regiment for some days; so I went to the medical director: "I am so-and-so, doctor, on leave of absence. If I can be of service, send me up as a nurse till I can rejoin my regiment." That night I went to "Springfield Landing," three miles below the grim, hostile batteries, — as near as peaceful vessels dare go. As we touched land at midnight, the air was full of thunder; and whirling among the stars went the lighted fuses of the slow-revolving bombs, high up toward the zenith, then dropping through a long, fire-lit arch to a deep explosion, — all this now close at hand: what we had been hearing on the remote bayou, fifty miles away.

Here began my week of hospital-work, — a week of most profound and soul-touching experiences, — a week when work went on from day-dawn to day-dawn almost without intermission; when new resources and new strength were developed in all who were there.

Without mattress or covering, I had been sleeping on the bare boards of the cabin, when the halting of the boat, and the roar of the fleet-guns in the river just ahead, awakened me. As the bow touched the shore, a slight, pleasant-faced gentleman, with nothing to denote his connection with the army but a little badge on his Panama-hat, came up the cabin-stairs.

"Where can I find Dr. L——, sir?"

"I am Dr. L——," was his answer; and I presented my credentials. The doctor was in charge of the hospital at the landing. There were tents pitched; but they were filled with stores or with other men: so, for the night, I remained aboard the steamer; and, in spite of the cannonade, slept well.

I arose at dawn, — it was Sunday, the 24th of May, — and took the first view by daylight of my new location. The river, I found, was here divided, — Prophet Island standing between the two branches of the stream. I could see the "Richmond" at the distance of about a mile and a half up the river, and was told that the remaining vessels of the fleet lay near her. Beyond the "Richmond" lay the threatening line of bluffs, on which were planted the rebel batteries; but from that distance they could not be seen.

Close at hand, the shore was so low as evidently to be covered by the river at high water. The soil gave evidence of having been lately submerged, though now it was dry. Dr. L——'s tents, two or three in number, were pitched in a grove of young saplings, in the rear of a great pile of ammunition and subsistence. Back of these, again, ran the road by which communication was maintained with the army. The "Kineo" lay at anchor a rod or two from shore; and up the bank a little way were tents, and three or four Parrott siege-guns of the largest caliber I have ever seen on wheels. The only building near was an old warehouse, which we tore to pieces for fuel.

Breakfast was cooked among the saplings; and there I first met my fellow-nurses. There were two stout corporals of a Maine regiment, good-natured and bovine; a round-faced corporal of another regiment; a stout battery-man — an ex-teamster from the Quincy quarries — of the Fourth Massachusetts regiment; the skipper of a West-India trading-brig, who had come from Bangor to try his hand at war; &c. Most of them were convalescents from Baton Rouge, not yet recovered enough to rejoin their regiments, but considered fit for hospital-duty. So great was the want of men, that the sick were almost taken from their beds and set to work. There was also a hospital-steward, — a good-looking, capable fellow, with his golden caduceus, embroidered upon green, just above his elbow. There was, besides, a functionary whom we called the commissary, whose business was to guard and deal out the stores.

A great battle might happen at any hour. Already many wounded had been brought in, and despatched to Baton Rouge, from the preliminary skirmishes; and it was high time for the doctor to complete his preparations. He collected us in line before him, and gave us his instructions. We were not to go from the landing : we were to pay most careful attention to the comfort of the wounded ; and, if we were detailed to go to Baton Rouge with boat-loads of them, there must be perfect kindness and faithfulness.

There was plenty to be done. We could hear the sound of heavy guns at the front ; and all the morning we were very busy pitching new tents. sweeping and policeing about the hospital, collecting fuel, and chopping down inconvenient trees. When I am with the regiment, owing to my profession, which is generally known, I am treated with some deference. Things have been made easy for me by the kindness of friends ; and I am spared many of the rough knocks to which the rank and file in general are exposed. Here, however, I was unknown. I stood among the rest simply a corporal of infantry. No one knew me as a clergyman ; we none of us knew each other's antecedents and expectations. We were briskly ordered here and there. I was glad to see that I passed among the others for a pretty stout fellow ; being set with the strongest to chop and dig and clean. I worked with a will ; and believe I established myself that first day, in the good opinion of the doctor and the steward, as a pretty tolerable hand. Most of the nurses being convalescents, a good deal fell to the share of the two or three of us who called ourselves well.

At noon, a number of sick arrived from the front.

We heard sharper firing. The "Kineo," weighing anchor, — her crew, who all the morning had been on deck, in clean, fresh dresses, stripping off their shirts, — began to make headway up stream to go into action. Presently we heard her eleven-inch gun close up under the batteries. During the afternoon, long trains of army-wagons took off commissary and ordnance stores; the useful mule-teams dragging through the light soil loads that would soon use up the stoutest horses. At the end of the afternoon, the medical director came up with Dr. F——, who is to be associated with Dr. L—— in the conduct of the hospital. With these gentlemen came ice, lemons, soft bread, wine, &c.; which we got up to the tents, then went to work vigorously on ice-houses. The medical director went to the front, and brought back word, at dark, that the "news is good; we are closing in on them; the assault is impending, and we must be ready."

Next day we finish our ice-houses. We get through, too, with our tent-pitching, — putting up two large pavilions, capable of holding about sixty wounded, stretched out at length, with comfort, and more than that with crowding. At noon came in more of the sick, and the first wounded man since my arrival. We carry him on his stretcher out under the trees, where it is shady and cool; and I, anxious to be broken in as soon as possible, kneel down by the side of the hospital steward to learn the operations of dressing. This man had been shot through the leg in a skirmish; not a severe hurt, as compared with wounds often received.

I moisten the bandages, dry and stiff with blood, until they unwind easily. We lay bare and gently wash the bullet-holes through the limb, apply fresh lint and clean bandages, and bring the man to rest under the tent. In the afternoon, we have arrivals of thirty or forty sick or wounded. The ambulances stop in the road; and we go down with stretchers, four men to each. Generally, the wounded are sadly wearied and jolted by the long ride over a rough road. They come with various hurts, — shot in body, head, legs, and arms. As gently as we can, we move them from the wagons to the stretchers; then from the stretchers again to the pallets on the floors of the tents.

It grew dark while they were arriving. We moistened their bandages, gave them iced lemonade and punch, and brought them toast and tea from the cook's. One was a stout German sergeant, shot through the foot accidentally by a comrade. We had numbers of such cases. Several had lost an arm, the stump being done up in bloody bandages; many had had a hand or foot badly shattered. By candle-light, the surgeons made their rounds. At this depot, all that was intended was to refresh the patients, and transfer them comfortably to the boats for Baton Rouge. There convenient hospitals were prepared, and surgeons to attend them. Here it was the design only to dress such wounds as needed it at once, and perform such operations as were immediately pressing.

This night, I saw a wound probed for the first time. The bullet had entered just above the knee. Dr. F came in with his probe, a fine instrument of steel, with a small ball of ivory at the end. I shrank from seeing it done, but thought I must accustom myself to it, or I should be able to do nothing at all. The patient was a brave, easy fellow, who started coolly, in the operation, to hold the light for the doctor, himself. The pain was too great for that : but still he was smiling and unflinching through the whole of it ; straightening up on his hands from his couch, and offering his leg to the instrument.

From evening it becomes night. The surgeons retire ; and one by one the nurses drop off, until at length, long past midnight, only two or three of us are left. The candles burn low ; the wounded sleep, or groan as their smarts and aches drive away slumber. Carefully and quietly we step from one to another, and soothe them as tenderly as we can. At last, we wake up some of the nurses who have slept ; and, expecting a hard day when the sun rises, lay down for a few hours' rest ourselves.

Tuesday morning, after all, opened with little to be done. Before I rose, the wounded we had been tending had been moved aboard a steamer, and were on their way to comfort. The ice-houses now were all filled. Among the stores were quantities of whiskey, wine, lemons, soft bread, lint, bandages, &c. The surgeons had their instruments in readiness ; the cooks had convenient kitchens, and huge boilers for making soup, tea, and coffee. Negroes were procured to sweep out the great tents, clear out the bloody bandages and cotton, and lay beds, sweet and fresh, for the next lot of sufferers. The doctors were kind, and wished us to rest while we could. During the forenoon, I slept; at noon, dined light on soft bread and tea (for, during this whole week, our fare was rather light for our work); got a drink of ice-water from a barrel in front of the commissary's, and was entirely fresh again. Bed-ticks in great quantity were on hand. From the quartermaster we got bales of hay, and stuffed the ticks; heaping up a great pile to use from. We got out mosquito-bars to protect the wounded from the flies; had pails, wash-basins, and sponges all in readiness; and, soon in the afternoon, the ambulances began to arrive.

The battle has not yet been fought. These are still only the victims of the preliminary skirmishes, and those who have been accidentally injured. The beds are spread in rows. The great hospital-tents stand one behind the other; the canvas between them, and, at either end, looped up high, so that the air can draw freely through. The beds lie in four long rows on the ground, from end to end, the outermost rows close down under the eaves, an aisle running down between. Beside ourselves, we have our stout negroes for help; and, one by one, the ambulances are emptied.

"Take them carefully, boys! Ambulance-driver, you are used to handling them. Get over from your seat in front, and manage the head of the poor prostrate fellow. Let one take the feet, as we slide him out; now a stout one, to catch him at the hips. Carefully, down upon the canvas! Stop groaning! Poor fellow! it is over."

Here is one with foot mashed by a piece of shell. This one is struck in the calf. Here is one whose leg is gone. The bloody swathings are hot and stiff. We will moisten them with ice-cold water. Here is one struck in the groin : the ball has gone through, and been cut out of the haunch behind. He lives, is bright, and may get well. This cavalry-man is shot clear through, from hip to hip. He is stripped, and the bullet-holes on each side are plain. He lives too. What will not the human body endure? A solid shot has struck this cannoneer in the bowels. Mortally wounded he is. The doctor takes off the broad piece of cloth that covers the hurt, revealing the horrible mangling; then replaces it. There is nothing for him but a dose of morphine to deaden the pain. They have been hit everywhere. Hardly a muscle or bone or fibre of the human body but has been struck in one or another of this unfortunate company, — lungs, shoulders and chest, arms and hands, neck, face, eyes; and, while I am moving a tall Zouave in his brilliant dress, the cloth upon his head drops off, as his shoulders are in my hands. The skull is cleft by a fragment of shell, apparently, deep down into the brain, whose inmost recesses are revealed in the bright sun. Yet he lives too !

All now are in the two tents. The ambulance-drivers go back to the cooks for their suppers; but our work is only begun. The doctors go rapidly from man to man. I follow Dr. L—— with a pail of water, soon red and thick with blood, with which to moisten the dressings. Quickly, but pleasantly and quietly, he lays bare the most hideous hurts. I catch the lesson from him. Do not let the patient see an over-anxious face, nor hear too deep sympathy in the voice, lest it should alarm. Be cheerful and tender, and let tone and look give as much encouragement as possible.

Dr. L—— has another assistant, — a gentleman in citizen's dress, of intellectual face, full of nerve, and ready-handed, — who kneels at one side of the doctor, as I do at the other, holding the instruments. The light is not bright, and I have little leisure for any thing but the wounds; yet I find time to study this man some. He is Barclay, a young minister; here as a delegate of the Christian Commission. In a day or two, I know him better. So we go from bed to bed, stepping carefully among bandaged shoulders, and bloody stumps of legs and arms, and faces pale as the swathings that wrap the head above. Generally, the most severe wounds are not apparently painful; the sufferer lying benumbed, I suppose, by the severing of important nerves. Lacerations of the hands and feet appear to cause most agony. Again we work on, until the candles burn low; holding ice here, bathing a limb or back there, or holding tea to pale lips here. It is morning again, when I arouse a sleeper to take his turn, and give me a chance to sleep.

Through Wednesday morning, we hear a fiercer cannonade than before. A few sick come in from the front during the forenoon; but these, and the wounded we had the night previous, are speedily sent to Baton Rouge. I catch a little sleep after dinner; and, when I awake, am set upon a dreadful task. It is to watch the cannoneer, wounded in the bowels. He was struck on Saturday. It is Wednesday evening, and he is still alive, but with his wound and whole body in a condition not to be described. He lies stripped for greater coolness, only covered with a netting. Somebody must watch beside him. He is delirious, but wants water and to be fanned; and, loathsome as he is, an attendant must be at his side. He tears the cloth from his horrible wound, and I must replace it. I must stand ready to catch his hands. He is decomposing like a corpse, although life yet remains. Toward midnight, he receives a still heavier dose of morphine, and I can leave. I hear that he died before morning.

While I have been at this task, much has been doing. Early after dark, word comes from the front, of the repulse and terrible loss of the storming party; and the surgeons are warned of the approach of a large number of wounded. We hear of the fall of generals and colonels, and rank and file without number; and close upon the heels of the intelligence follow the ambulances, loaded as never before with hastily dressed wounded from the field-hospitals in front. It is about ten o'clock when I go aboard the "Iberville" at the landing; to which the ambulances are transferring their loads at once, instead of leaving them first in our tents. As I enter the cabin-door, the long, handsome saloon, from end to end, is filled with the victims of the battle just fought. From the rich, bronze chandeliers, light falls upon a ghastly sight, — all the ghastlier from con-

trast with the elegance about. I can hardly step among
the prostrate and gory company. And so they lie all
through the long perspective, the great mirror at the
farther end repeating it all anew; the stains upon their
wrappings, about heads and limbs and bodies, red as the
figures of the rich carpet upon which they lie.

At the farther end, just in front of the mirror, lie a
Zouave major, two colonels, an adjutant of a Maine
regiment, then the brave and unfortunate young colonel
of the Massachusetts Forty-ninth. He lost a leg at
Ball's Bluff. Now he is shot through the other foot
and through the wrist. Only twenty-three! I watch
his face and figure, and think how Dr. Holmes would
write him down a Brahmin of the Brahmins. There is
no sign of suffering upon his well-cut, knightly features.
He meets pain with calm dignity. His tall, slight figure
is stretched at length upon his couch, — the slender,
white foot showing out, bandaged up about the instep.
The officers all are patient and brave. One colonel is
shot through the face, the other through the arm and
back, the adjutant in the knee, the Zouave in the body.
Their fine uniforms are stained with battle-gore, and
ruffled by the long ambulance-ride, — gold lace and
brilliant trimmings all torn and cut to reach the hurt.

There is much to be done. Dr. L—— and Barclay
are there, and but few others. There are many thirsty
ones, — many whose wounds feel as if a burning brand
were being applied, and who call for water. Barclay
is attending to these wants; and, besides, is applying
the stores of the Sanitary Commission, of which he is

also an agent. I do not know where he keeps them; but it seems as if he must have them in some way compressed into his pocket, so readily does he produce clean white garments, pillows, and towels, whenever they are needed.

Here on a pallet lies a German corporal — Philbert his name — belonging to a New-York regiment. An officer near says he is the literary man of the regiment, a refined scholar and gentleman, who has gone into the ranks to help his adopted country. He lies with a painful wound through his wrist, — brave, cheerful, and modest. He tells how he carried a fascine in the first line, in front of the stormers; and how all were swept down in the whirlwind of canister and grape they met as they came within range. Some are benumbed and stupefied, some groaning in great pain; but often I find cheerful, smiling faces.

The drink gives out, and I go ashore to refill the pails. Just as I step out into the open air, I hear loud shrieks and cries. I hurry on to the Levee. The moon, nearly full, is now low in the west; and I see clearly by its light an ambulance, just arrived, about which an escort of Zouaves — in uniforms of white and scarlet, set off with silver lace — are hurrying. In the throng, too, are more soberly-dressed ambulance-men, — all covered with dust. A wounded man is just being taken out. I hurry to the spot, finding Barclay there, of course; for he is always where there is suffering. He whispers to me that it is a famous general of division. Dr. F——, who is directing matters, catches my eye in the crowd, and sends me off for a stimulant. It is put to the general's lips; and I follow the litter aboard Admiral Farragut's despatch-steamer, which is to convey him to New Orleans. I catch sight of his agonized face in the moonlight, and recognize him as the same general in whose tent I had sat on one occasion, rather more than a year before, in the camp at Port Royal.

I left him groaning and shrieking beneath the awning on the deck of the little steamer, and went up again to the tents to procure the refreshments and other articles I was in search off; then returned to the cabin of the "Iberville." It was now far toward daylight. The surgeons had all retired, except one who had volunteered for the time from one of the ships of the fleet. There was still plenty to be done; but I waked up some of the sleepers, and lay down for a few hours' rest.

I could not sleep long; and, soon after sunrise, was about again. I ate my light breakfast of bread and tea, and went again to the "Iberville's" cabin. She was loaded above and below now, and about to start upon her voyage; but, while she waited, the surgeons and nurses were at work. Ambulances were from time to time arriving, bringing now many of the fine black fellows of Nelson's regiment, which had passed the great test so well the day before.

The attempt to storm Port Hudson was unsuccessful; but something was done then to forward our cause, because it was on this day that black soldiers underwent their ordeal. Side by side with white troops, they were exposed to a hot fire, and bore themselves well. Col.

8*

Higginson, in South Carolina, has had his men under fire, to be sure; but his fighting has been of an irregular sort. Here, for the first time, they were exposed in a pitched battle; and their praise is in every mouth. I am glad I can write that the wounded blacks received all possible attention. They lay about the steamer wherever it was airy and pleasant. The surgeons were attentive. Barclay poured out the stores of the Sanitary and Christian Commissions without stint, and we nurses did all we could. I moistened many a black fellow's wound; and where, as sometimes happened, they were stripped, that the surgeons might more readily reach their injuries, I adjusted the screens that kept off insects and the sun. They were never otherwise than full of patience and gratitude.

I also washed the wounds and the faces of the officers at the end of the cabin, and happened to be on hand to help in a very trying surgical operation. I held the leg of the young adjutant while Dr. L—— cut a bullet out of the bones of the knee, in which it had become deeply embedded. It was a painful and critical operation. A few days before, I should have fainted at the sight; but, in such scenes, the sensibilities become blunted.

Every available foot of space now aboard the "Iberville," above and below, was filled with wounded men; and four nurses, I for one, were detailed to go with the boat to Baton Rouge. All were fed, above and below. We stood at hand with wet sponges and cooling drinks; and, meantime, the steamer with her sad freight slipped rapidly down the fifteen miles to Baton Rouge. Hospitals were prepared at the old Arsenal Buildings; and, as the boat rounded to, the intrenchments and banks everywhere were crowded with people.

The boat was soon emptied of its freight. I piled up the beds, as they were vacated, on one side of the cabin; and then had a little leisure to go ashore, and see a room or two of the permanent hospital. They looked neat and comfortable. The rooms were airy; the beds clean, and protected by mosquito-bars; the patients soon washed, and provided with food and fresh clothing. The steamer was presently on her way back. I managed to get a good dinner aboard; then spread a bed on the cabin-floor, and got an hour or two of welcome and needed sleep. I had worked very hard, and, I believe, gained the good-will of the surgeons. Besides, one or two old patients of mine, whom I had nursed in typhoid fever, had been at the landing, and, I believe, had spoken a good word for me. More and more responsibility was put upon me.

As soon as I had returned, the hospital-steward told me I was to take charge of removing a large number of wounded to the boat from the tents, who had been brought down from the field during our trip. Here were my negroes, here the nurses I could have, and here the stretchers. I went right to work. I had gained confidence, found my strength was good, and therefore was not afraid to handle even the worst cases. I dared to take hold of the stumps when it was necessary, the pierced hips, and lacerated shoulders. I had found that a quick, steady movement caused the least pain.

About dark, — this was Thursday, — the task was accomplished, but only to make room for another; for now a longer string of ambulances than ever had come. The surgeons had gone to bed exhausted, and could not be disturbed. The hospital-steward was not to be found; and upon me came the responsibility of getting them all housed, fed, and cared for during the night. I had the beds laid in as good order as possible, working as I never worked before; then superintended, as well as I could, the removal of the men from the ambulances to the pallets upon the ground. It seemed as if we never had received a lot so dreadfully mangled: we certainly never received so many. With as much despatch as possible, I assigned to each his place. Commissary-teams were waiting for the ambulances to get out of the way; and we had almost to jump and run among the closely packed crowd on the floor, in the dim candle-light. Outsiders, some of them officers, came in, but often hindered more than they helped, by misplaced sensibility, or unreasonable assumption of authority. The lightly wounded were to be put in the less accessible places under the eaves, as requiring least attention; the graver cases were to have the airiest beds; and the bodies of those who had bled to death in the ambulances had a place assigned to them in a tent outside. Barclay was at my right hand; a good man indeed. Together we took hasty counsel as to moving and making comfortable the more desperately injured. How could we take hold here so as not to jar the shattered lungs? and how, with this heavy, tall fellow, terribly hurt in the groin, — how could I get my hands under the hips, so as to lift him most easily? We worked hour after hour, the sweat starting from every pore, that hot, moon-lit night, until every inch of available space was packed, and all were fed.

I do not know how many regiments were represented. There were officers of all grades. A colonel shot through the hand: a captain shot in the neck; and another, a gentleman, in the midst of his suffering, his elegant dress dusty and gory. I was hoarse with giving directions in the hubbub, and worn out with want of sleep. Toward daylight again, I found a place to lie down.

I happened to lie down in the tent where Barclay kept his stores; and, when I awoke in the morning, he was there. He never appeared to need sleep. We had an interesting half-hour's talk. I told him about watching with the cannoneer, whose whole body was far gone with decay, and full of worms, although life yet lingered. Was it not almost a barbarity *not* to put him into the final sleep? Then came up the case of Napoleon, and the fever patients of his army in Syria. They, too, were sick to death; sure to become a prey to the Turk: was it so monstrous for him to propose to put them quickly and smoothly out of life? From that we got on to the question of suicide, and spoke of Godwin and French thinkers, and of Epietctus, and sages of old, who permitted such flight from life. "If the house smokes, leave it." We thought life was too sacred a thing for man to touch. God gave it: let him take it away, when it is time.

I got up from the ground before Barclay, soaked with sweat, and with dust and blood adhering everywhere. I apologized for my appearance; for it was my only shirt. He gave me another out of the Sanitary-Commission stores, in which I once more felt decent.

This was Friday, — a day much like the previous ones. Besides the "Iberville," there were two or three other steamers to take the wounded; and, one after another, they went down stream freighted. During the day, we had a fine shower, which cooled the air. To dress a wound is no slight operation. To undo gaping injuries, wash them, stanch the blood; then do them up neatly, and feel they are safe, — all this, one does not reach at once.

My hospital-service, however, was coming to a close. Saturday morning, began to arrive the Fifty-second Regiment. During the fortnight I had spent on my journey, and at Springfield Landing, they had performed a march of one hundred and thirty miles; being part of the guard of the immense train in which the negroes and a vast portion of the wealth of the Têche and Opelousas neighborhoods were brought to the seaboard. That work had been accomplished; and now, at the end of May, they had been hurried up the river to re-enforce the besieging army. Saturday afternoon, when the regiment passed the hospital on its way to the front, I bade Barclay and my old mates good-by, and fell in with the colors in my old place.

CHAPTER XIII.

BATTLE.

JUNE 2, 1863. — Before Port Hudson, within easy cannon-range. This morning, we are not marching or fighting. We lie encamped in a wood, at the edge of a clearing, across which the rebel works are in plain sight, at the distance of a few hundred yards. The boys, who venture only a few rods from here to the edge of the clearing, find the shots of the rebel sharpshooters falling about them : their shells frequently strike in and about our camp. A piece of one has fallen within a few yards of me, breaking three muskets out of a stack that stood in the line. Day and night, our batteries are firing. Every few minutes, and at times more frequently, the earth-shaking roar of pieces of very large caliber makes the whole region tremble. Hardiker and I have built a little booth of boughs, whose roof may be taken off at any moment by a rebel missile. Two or three times last night, the earth flew to the right and left of the dead tree-trunk at whose foot we were resting.

June 11. — We feel perfectly at home now in these woods. We were here some days, once in a while shifting our camp to avoid the shells; then came the episode of the march to Clinton and back. I do not mean to write much about this; for the readers and the inditer of these notes have had enough of hard marching. Let these few words suffice. A body of our cavalry had been attacked, and very roughly handled, in the neighborhood of this place of Clinton; and Gen. Paine was sent out with a force to catch and chastise this body, if possible.

The force, consisting of regiments detached from this and that brigade, with some artillery and a large body of cavalry, left camp in the forest here about four o'clock one morning. How hot and dusty it grew! We began by taking the wrong road, which gave us extra distance of five or six miles; then, in the end, we went by the longest route. The first day, at noon, the heat became perfectly intolerable. Several were nearly killed by its power, and we were forced to halt until night. Thenceforth we marched for the most part at night; but the dust was deep, the nights hot, and the water often poor. At length, at dawn one morning, we halted within two or three miles of Clinton, to hear from the cavalry in advance that the foe had fled. Back we came, therefore, dragging wearily into our old camp through all the dust and heat, tired in every bone, every fibre of clothing soaked and resoaked in perspiration; having, in the course of four days, gone some fifty or sixty miles. We hope it was our last march. God send it may be so! for it is too much for men.

After our return, we gave a day or two to grateful

rest. Abundant rations were drawn, among them a quantity of soft bread, — nothing but dry and rather sour flour-bread; but how we jumped at it!

We are waiting now in the woods for something else. The sound of guns is constant to us here; and, at the "front" (a short walk from us), scarcely a minute passes without a report: for there you can catch the cannonade of the fleet, and that from the other approaches of the army. In the evening, from every quarter, can be seen the dropping of shells into the rebel works, — the fuses of the bombs whirling through the air, — and the sudden lighting-up of the explosions.

A formidable battery of ship's guns has opened, within a few days, not far from us. My first visit to it was in the evening. Bivins and I slung our canteens (for we never miss an opportunity of going for water), and started down the blind, obstructed cart-track which leads out of the woods. Every few minutes came in the heavy crash of the Dahlgrens we were going to see; that and the lighter reports of guns farther off. We were soon out on the plain, where the battery is placed. To the right of it ran a hedge; behind which, screened from the rebel riflemen, lay a regiment, stationed there to protect the guns against a sudden dash of the enemy.

It is now quite dark; but, in the starlight, we can see the outlines of the sand-work, behind which the guns are ranged. The rebel intrenchments are, from quarter to half a mile away, in front of us. We can see three or four large fires burning within them. Volumes of flame and smoke roll up among the trees, and the soldiers about us think they can make out the figures of men standing by the glare. As often as once a minute, from the east, where lies a huge New-York battery; from the right, which Weitzel holds; or over on the opposite side from us, where lies the fleet in the river, — as often as once in a minute, like heat-lightning, flashes a cannon; then, in a few seconds, comes the roar; then another light within the fortress, as the shell explodes.

Now a " Dahlgren " in our battery here is discharged. How fierce and sullen! I must have a nearer view: so I make my way in behind the earth-work itself, and stand with the sailors, who are detached from duty on ship-board to manage these great fellows. Each gun stands on a broad platform, sloping from rear to front to prevent the recoil of the piece from sending it too far back. They are part of the broadside of the " Richmond; " and have already done good service at the taking of the forts, and the running of the Port-Hudson batteries in March.

" Ready there at No. 2 !" says the officer in charge. The crew of " No. 2 " stand back, and I brace myself for the concussion. A sailor jerks a lanyard, and it is done. It is no light field-piece, remember; but one of war's grimmest monsters. Clash go my teeth together, my bones almost rattle; then follows the hungry, ravening shriek of the shell, which breaks forth like a horrible bird of prey to devour the whole world. It sweeps hoarsely toward the enemy's line; then I hear it go " thud-thud !" through some obstruction. In a moment, the air beyond is lit up with its bursting; and the sound roars back to us. — to us, now enveloped in the sulphurous cloud that wraps the whole neighborhood.

The rebels now very seldom answer our artillery. Before we went to Clinton, occasionally they opened on us with shell. If we lighted fires at night, betraying our position in the woods, presently we could hear the shells come humming toward the light like great dor-bugs of a summer-night. Hum-m-m! then a burst, and a dash of heavy iron, "thump" upon the ground in the midst of the camp. Lately, however, there has been no firing, except by their riflemen.

June 16. — I write in a corner of a ravine, close within rifle-range of the works at Port Hudson. The Fifty-second Regiment are holding an advanced position here, and, ever since daylight of the morning of the 14th, have lived in the midst of a rain of rifle-balls. At the bottom of the little ravine, I am secure; but if I should put my head up to the surface, climbing up the bank six or eight feet, I should be in the midst of flying bullets, and a fair mark for the rebel sharpshooters who are close at hand. Our brigade is thrown out into the very teeth of the enemy, on ground our troops have never before occupied. This little corner is occupied by the color-guard. If I go to the company, I must go stooping or crawling on my stomach; I must run from a stump to a trunk, and from that to a clump of bushes, and hear all the time the "zip" and "hum" of the rifle-balls.

We have had a battle. Not quite a week ago, we began to hear of it. Some of the regiments which were to be engaged were told of it; and Gen. Paine, who

was to have an important command, made speeches
among his men, and instructed them in the use of hand-
grenades. In the woods, parties of men were busy,
cutting fascines; and bags of cotton, as large as a man
could comfortably carry, were piled up near the approaches to the enemy's works. We knew nothing
certain, however, until Saturday. (It is now Tuesday.)
Toward the end of that afternoon, the explicit orders
came. The assault was to be made the next morning,
and our regiment was to have a share in it. We were
not to go home without the baptism of fire and blood.

Before dark, we were ordered into line, and stacked
our arms. Each captain made a little speech. "No
talking in the ranks; no flinching. Let every one see
that his canteen is full, and that he has hard bread
enough for a day. That is all you will carry beside gun
and equipments." We left the guns in stack, polished,
and ready to be caught on the instant; and lay down
under the trees. At midnight came the cooks with coffee and warm food. Soon after came the order to move;
then, slowly and with many halts, nearly four hundred
strong, we took up our route along the wood-paths.
Many other regiments were also in motion. The forest
was full of Rembrandt pictures, — a bright blaze under
a tree, the faces and arms of soldiers all aglow about it;
the wheel of an army-wagon, or the brass of a cannon, lit
up; then the gloom of the wood, and the night shutting
down about it.

At length, it was daybreak; and, with every new
shade of light in the east, a new degree of energy was

imparted to the cannonade. As we stood at the edge of the wood, it was roar on all sides. In a few minutes, we were in motion again. We crossed a little bridge over a brook thickly covered with cotton to conceal the tramp of men, and noise of wheels ; climbed a steep pitch, and entered a trench or military road cut through a ravine, passing some freshly made rifle-pits and batteries. We were now only screened from the rebel works by a thin hedge. Here the rifle-balls began to cut keen and sharp through the air about us ; and the cannonade, as the east now began to redden, reached its height, — a continual deafening uproar, hurling the air against one in great waves, till it felt almost like a wall of rubber, bounding and rebounding from the body, — the great guns of the "Richmond," the siege-Parrotts, the smaller field-batteries ; and, through all, the bursting of the shells within the rebel lines, and the keen, deadly whistle of well-aimed bullets. A few rods down the military road, the column paused. The work of death had begun ; for ambulance-men were bringing back the wounded : and, almost before we had time to think we were in danger, I saw one of our men fall back into the arms of his comrades, shot dead through the chest. The banks of the ravine rose on either side of the road in which we had halted : but just here the trench made a turn ; and in front, at the distance of five or six hundred yards, we could plainly see the rebel rampart, red in the morning-light as with blood, and shrouded in white vapor along the edge as the sharpshooters behind kept up an incessant discharge. I believe I felt no sensation of fear, nor do I think those about me did. Wilson and Hardiker carried the flags, and their faces were cheerful and animated. I thanked God that Sunday morning that I was in perfect strength in every limb for that day's most solemn service, — service not to be rendered in any peaceful temple, but amid grime of powder, and sweat of blood : nevertheless His service, and that which should bring about for Him the acceptable things.

Our brigadier is with us at the front; and now, calling the colonel, the two soldierly figures climb the bank of the ravine, and take a narrow survey of the ground. In a moment, the order comes. We are to move up this rough path to the right, then advance out from the shelter of the trees into the open space before the fortifications; deploying as skirmishers meanwhile, and making our way through the fire to a closer position. We climb up the path. I go with my rifle between Wilson and Hardiker; keeping nearest the former, who carries the national flag. In a minute or two, the column has ascended, and is deploying in a long line, under the colonel's eye, on the open ground. The rebel engineers are most skilful fellows. Between us and the brown earth-heap which we are to try to gain to-day, the space is not wide; but it is cut up in every direction with ravines and gullies. These were covered, until the parapet was raised, with a heavy growth of timber; but now it has all been cut down, so that in every direction the fallen tops of large trees interlace, trunks block up every passage, and brambles are growing over the whole. It

is out of the question to advance here in line of battle ;
it seems almost out of the question to advance in any
order : but the word is given, "Forward !" and on we go.
Know that this whole space is swept by a constant patter
of balls : it is really a " leaden rain." We go crawling
and stooping : but now and then before us rises in
plain view the line of earth-works, smoky and sulphurous with volleys ; while all about us fall the balls, now
sending a lot of little splinters from a stump, now knocking the dead wood out of the old tree-trunk that is shel-
tering me, now driving up a cloud of dust from a little
knoll, or cutting off the head of a weed just under the
hand as with an invisible knife. I see one of our best
captains carried off the field, mortally wounded, shot
through both lungs, — straight, bright-eyed, though so
sadly hurt, supported by two of his men ; and now
almost at my side, in the color-company, one soldier is
struck in the hand, and another in the leg. "Forward !"
is the order. We all stoop ; but the colonel does not
stoop : he is as cool as he was in his tent last night,
when I saw him drink iced lemonade. He turns now
to examine the ground, then faces back again to direct
the advance of this or that flank. Wilson springs on
from cover to cover, and I follow close after him. It is
hard work to get the flag along : it cannot be carried in
the air ; and we drag it and pass it from hand to hand
among the brambles, much to the detriment of its folds.
The line pauses a moment. Capt. Morton, who has
risen from a sick-bed to be with his command, is coolly
cautioning his company. The right wing is to remain

in reserve, while the left pushes still farther forward. The major is out in front of us now. He stands upon a log which bridges a ravine, — a plain mark for the sharpshooters, who overlook the position, not only from the parapet, but from the tall trees within the rebel works. Presently we move on again, through brambles and under charred trunks, tearing our way, and pulling after us the colors; creeping on our bellies across exposed ridges, where bullets hum and sing like stinging bees; and, right in plain view, the ridge of earth, its brow white with incessant volleys.

Down this slope, and it will do. The color-guard is some rods in advance of the company, and may pause. I hear cheering. A ridge hides the space in front of the works from which it comes; and I tell Wilson I must creep up, and see the charge.

"Better not," he says. "We will go where our duty lies; but we had better run no risk beyond that."

He is wiser than I. While he speaks, I have partially raised myself to climb forward to the point of view. Balls are striking close by me. I have become a mark to sharpshooters in the trees, and lie down again to be safe. The color-guard are under orders not to fire, except when the colors are especially threatened. My piece is loaded and capped; but I can only be shot at, without returning the discharge. Down into our little nook now come tumbling a crowd of disorganized, panting men. They are part of a New-York regiment, who, on the crest just over us, have been meeting with very severe loss. They say their dead and dying are heaped up there.   We believe it; for we can hear them, they are so near: indeed, some of those who come stumbling down are wounded; some have their gun-stocks broken by shot, and the barrels bent, while they are unharmed.   They are frightened and exhausted, and stop to recover themselves: but presently their officers come up, and order them forward again.   From time to time, afterwards, wounded men crawl back from their position a few yards in front of where we are, — one shot through the ankles, who, however, can crawl on his hands and knees: one in the hand; one with his blouse all torn about his breast, where a ball has struck him, yet he can creep away.   Looking up toward the top of our little ravine, I had seen Company D climb-ing forward; the well-known heads and faces coming into sight for the moment as they climbed over an obstruction, then going down again into the bushes, — Wivers active as a squirrel; McGill with his old black hat pulled down about his ears, as if it were a snowstorm he was out in.   They disappear; but soon I see the head of Bivins making rapid way back-ward.

"What is the matter, Bivins?"

"Sergt. Rogers is shot."

"Killed?"

"No: through the thigh, well up; but, we think, not fatally.   I am going for a stretcher."

"Look out for yourself meantime!" I shout to him; thinking of his bright young wife and little boy, who would come to sad grief enough, if that honest head,

9

appearing and disappearing among the tangled thickets, should be brought low by a rebel marksman.

It is now noon and after. The sun is intolerably hot, and we have no sufficient shade. That, however, is nothing for us who are unhurt; but we hear of poor wounded men lying without shelter, among them Gen. Paine, whom the ambulance-men cannot yet reach on account of the enemy's fire. We begin to know that the attack has failed. Toward the end of the afternoon, at considerable risk, I make my way to Company D. They are on the brow of an eminence, on a flat plateau, just even with the rebel gun-barrels, almost without shelter; all lying flat on their backs and stomachs, the flying balls keeping up a constant drone and hum just above them. Rogers ventured to stand up, and was shot almost at once. The men told how they had looked over the hill-brow, and seen the charge, — the fruitless dash at the impenetrable obstacles, — the volley from the breastworks, the fall of scores. We know nothing certainly. There are rumors, thick as the rifle-balls, of this general killed, that regiment destroyed, and successful attempts elsewhere. The sun goes down on this day of blood. We have lost several killed, and several more wounded, and have done all we were called upon to do. The colonel tells us we have been cool, prudent, and brave. We have not been as much exposed as some other regiments, and our loss has not been large. The fire, however, seemed very hot, and close at hand; and the wonder to us all is, that no more fell. Darkness settles down; shots are received and returned, but only at random now; and, ever and anon, from the batteries goes tearing through the air a monstrous shell, with a roar like a rushing railroad-train, then an explosion putting every thing for the moment in light.

At dusk, I creep back to the ravine, where I am to sleep. I have been awake since midnight, and almost every moment since has been one of excitement; first the anticipation, then the reality, of a pitched battle. What a day for these remote plains and woods! The little frightened birds I have seen fly to and fro, painfully shaken, I must believe, in their delicate frames by the concussion of the air during the cannon volleys; for I have felt it sensibly. So the green, harmless lizards, whose beauty and lithesome movement I have loved to watch, — these I have seen to-day, when I have looked up from my covert, peering about curiously, and running to and fro to find out the occasion of this uproar and jar, so suddenly come to disturb their haunts. For food to-day, I have had two or three hard crackers and cold potatoes. We have no blankets: so down I lie to sleep as I can on the earth, without covering; and, before morning, am chilled through with the dew and coldness of the air.

CHAPTER XIV.

THE WOLF AT BAY.

OUR brigade is thrown forward, as Gen. Banks says, "upon the threshold of the enemy's fortifications," and have it for their duty to maintain an incessant skirmish, day and night, with those sharp-eyed fellows just opposite.

Monday the heat is intense, and we have but little shelter. I fare hard; for I must draw rations with my company, and yet must remain with the colors, which are still in the ravine. Toward the evening of Monday, I work my way out to our cooks. One must go cautiously, stooping and creeping, and, when the balls whistle sharp, hiding till the riflemen look some other way. I gain, at length, the shelter of the woods behind, where lie unburied dead from the field, and piles of stretchers yet bloody with their burdens of wounded men. Each one of the color-guard to-night must watch. My watch is at midnight. I profess to love Nature, and in that love "hold communion with her visible forms." "For my gayer hours," I have indeed found that she has a "voice of gladness." To-night, my musings are darker. Certainly, O outer world! with a smile and deep eloquence of beauty do you glide into the soldier's musings, and steal away their sharpness.

I climbed up from the ravine, and sat alone, upon the hill on the field, under the starlight. It was a sweet night, and only once or twice came to my sense the taint of unburied slain. For the rest, all was pure. In a half-comic way, the whippoorwill changed his song into "Whipped you well, whipped you well!" I will never believe the bull-frogs that night croaked any thing but "Rebs, rebs!" and the jeering owls hooted out from the tree-tops, "What can *you* do-o-o?" All about the horizon, fringing the starlit space of blue, a storm was gathering; and behind the black clouds shook the lightning, like the menacing finger of an almighty power threatening doom to this obstinate stronghold. 'Twas like that, and 'twas like the vision seen, in days of romance, by King Arthur, — the sword "Excalibur" brandished by the phantom arm out of the lake.

June 17 — We are still in the front of the advance, living in dens and caves of the earth, maintaining our incessant skirmish, and occasionally losing men from the regiment. We go unwashed, uncombed, unshaven, creeping and stooping, with no baggage but the clothes on our backs, and they torn everywhere by brambles, and sometimes by shot. My only portfolio now is my cartridge-box, where I find room for a few sheets, and my pencil, among my sixty rounds, writing my record upon its broad leathern flap. This afternoon, there has been a flag of truce; during which they have buried dead, and even removed wounded men, who have lain on the field since Sunday! It is now Wednesday. Company D has assisted in burying a hundred and fourteen corpses.. I have just seen Cyrus Stowell, who tells me a terrible story. The decomposition of the bodies was so advanced, that the flesh slipped from the arms as our men tried to raise them, the heads fell away from the trunks sometimes, and the worms crawled from the dead upon the hands of the living! Unspeakably dreadful!

The rebels now use little artillery against us, but mostly rifles. Tremendous fellows they are. During the flag of truce this afternoon, plenty of them have been in plain sight—slovenly-looking butternuts—about the few tents and clumps of old buildings inside their parapet, and, indeed, in the open space between the two armies.

I have written about the assault of the 14th inst. Never come to a private soldier to pass judgment on a military act; for his horizon is too circumscribed to comprehend the circumstances. But the judgment of us, the rank and file, upon the matter, is this, — let it go for what it is worth, — that the men did their part: they showed willingness and bravery, but it was misdirected. Our men could see the charging regiments begin their rush, way back by an old chimney to our left here, — too far, too far, by a long distance, considering the difficult nature of the ground to be traversed. We heard the poor fellows' cheers as they started; but the rebs heard it too, and could be seen rushing to the

point of their works, against which the assaulting regiments were to dash. Their attention was attracted by
our unnecessary demonstrations, and our men received
more terrible volleys. The result was, about fifteen
hundred lost to us, by the last accounts.

We advanced in the battle as skirmishers, as I have
written ; and when the roar and heat were over, and the
tide of Federal energy and valor had ebbed again from
off the field, — leaving it wet with red pools, and strewn
with bloody drift, — it was given to our brigade to stay
in our steps, to hold the tangled ravines and slopes
we had conquered, under the daily and nightly volleys
of the Mississippi, Alabama, and Arkansas regiments,
who, we hear, hold the breast-work in our front.
Now and then we lose a man, killed or wounded ; but
we believe our loss would have been quadrupled, were
it not that our colonel has handled his command so
prudently and skilfully.

So far, my hands have no stain of human blood upon
them. Our rifles are always close at hand, loaded, to
be ready against any sortie, or if we should suddenly
have to charge. The regiment, generally, have prac-
tised much against the sand-bags and loop-holes of the
enemy's parapet ; but we do not fire until some hostile
hand seems likely to get the flag out of Wilson's grasp.

Until within a day or two, my situation has been
hard. I draw my rations with Company D, and they
have been posted at some distance from the ravine of
the color-guard. I could not always go for my food
at the right time, — sometimes could not go at all : at

any rate, it was always at a risk; for the only path was the obstructed, bullet-swept track leading from our ravine to the woods in the rear. Irregularity in eating, abstinence, exposure to the heat of burning days and the night-damps, have rather affected my condition. To the sights of war we have all become used, and can see the worst without sickening. Every day, gaping wounds and mangled death are borne past us, on stretchers, out of the rifle-pits and trenches. The surgeons and chaplain remain at the old camp in the woods which we left the midnight preceding the assault, and that has become a city of refuge for the sick. One tired boy after another has gone there, from the heat and damp at the front, until the companies have grown smaller than ever. The march from the Courtableau to Brashear City brought down numbers. Numbers have fallen sick here, so that our company has scarcely more than twenty on duty; and other companies are nearly as much reduced.

Though we are sick and worn, the general is determined we shall work while we remain. Early, Saturday the 20th, just before daylight, word came to us to march; whither, we knew not. We stole out quietly, so as not to attract the attention of the enemy; and marched to the general's head-quarters, some three miles in our rear. It turned out that a train of one hundred and forty wagons was going into the country for forage. We were to be its escort; and, while we stood in line, two pieces of light artillery and a body of cavalry came up, who were to help us.

On any large map, a short distance from Port Hudson, to the north-east, you will see a little village called Jackson. It was near that village that we halted at noon. Here two well-travelled roads crossed each other, near which were situated the two plantations from which the forage was to be taken. The colonel rode out to see the barns, and to post his guards to prevent surprise. We stacked arms near the crossing of the roads, and went into the shade close by to eat our scanty dinner. We found we had come to a pleasant region. The land rolled up into fine swells, which had been cleared of forest in great part, giving place to wide-spreading corn-fields, where the corn was already tall, and with ears large and well filled out. The landscape had a rich, cultivated aspect; looking not unlike a farming region in New York in August.

The colonel soon made his dispositions. Half a mile to the left, half the train of wagons waited their turn to load up; their white tops in plain view across the intervening fields. To the right, about the same distance from us, the remainder of the train stood upon another farm. We had just begun to open our haversacks, when "crack, crack!" we began to hear a heavy volley of rifle-shots. The Philistines were upon us. In an instant came the summons, "Battalion!" and we flew to our pieces. Pickets came galloping in from the outposts. The story is, that two rebel regiments and a body of horse bivouacked the night before at the farm on the right, where the teams are loading. The artillerymen are at their pieces; and all over the field, to the

skirts of the distant woods, squads of cavalry are seen
on the gallop, — most of them Grierson's famous men.
Presently the wagons come back in the wildest confusion, pell-mell, helter-skelter. The mules are in full
gallop, some with, some without drivers; over ditches
and fences, crash through groves of young pines, over
logs and stumps. Sometimes the body is jarred off
the wheels; sometimes one mule has broken loose,
leaving three behind, with the broken harness dragging
about them. The negro-drivers yell, and brandish
their whips. All is perfect uproar and panic.

The enemy appear in considerable numbers, swarming about the house and barns of a plantation. From a
little knoll, close by our position, the artillery open
a brisk fire of shell upon them, which does them great
damage, and throws them into as much disorder as the
wagons they have sought to seize. Two of our companies, thrown out as skirmishers, keep up a firing of
rifles, — the colonel, meantime, on the knoll, close at
hand to the battery, and the main body of the regiment,
which is supporting it, is surrounded by cavalry-men
and officers, who gallop up and away every instant.
His face has as cool and pleasant a look as ever, — the
calm and undisturbed spot in the midst of the panic.
We stand leaning on our pieces, ready for any thing
that may turn up.   •

Wouvermans, the old Dutch painter, used to take
battles for his favorite subjects. I have looked over
plates after his pictures; and this scene was precisely
one of Wouvermans' skirmishes, — the same confusion

and panic, a similar landscape, a lovely summer's day, and the encounter in the midst; infantry skirmishing, cavalry charging with drawn sabres, the snap of rifles from the distant woods, the rush of animals and fugitives to get out of danger. It was soon over. Some eight or ten fell on our side among the cavalry; and we have heard that a considerably larger number of the enemy were slain by the cannon. These were extremely well served, and probably saved us from being overpowered by a superior force.

The colonel judged it prudent to return at once. A few of the wagons had had time to load; some were broken, some had gone galloping on toward the Federal camp. The outposts were recalled, and we took up a backward line of march. We had proceeded five or six miles; when suddenly it was "halt" again, and word came back that the column was beset front and rear. Of the infantry, four men were detailed for a guard to each wagon; while the cavalry and cannon hastened forward to the front, from which we began to hear firing. It looked critical. Our term of service was within three weeks of its expiration, and we were all in danger of being taken prisoners. The imperturbable colonel rides along with cavalry and battery officers. "Can we not get a courier in for re-enforcements?" I hear one say. "We shall be enough for them, I guess, if we can only concentrate." We all feel confidence, make sure of our guns, put on fresh caps, and leave the hammer at half-cock. Then we go forward, and that is the *last of it.*

In the evening at ten o'clock, after we are in the camp once more in a grove of trees, I hear the colonel give results. It seems the rebs did capture some sixty of our wagons in the last attack. Their drivers were frightened, and had not obeyed orders. Moreover, the cavalry were unmanageable; and mules and wagons fell an easy prey, when a smart body of rebs dashed out of an ambuscade, and swept like a whirlwind through our long, straggling line. They had nothing to match our cannon. If it had not been for them, we might all have been on the way to Richmond.

Tired to death, almost worn out to start with, covered with a paste of perspiration and dust, it was hard to be waked up at midnight, just after we had fallen asleep, and be marched right back again into the trenches and rifle-pits, to press on the siege.

June 25. — The next day, — Sunday, — when we found life enough to open our dust-filled eyes and crawl about a little, we found the engineers, during the previous twenty-four hours, had been pushing matters. Just by us here is a bank, covered with trees and bushes, and really very much exposed to the enemy's fire. We often venture to pause, however, in the brush, and look at their earthworks, which can be seen from this point to advantage. Here I stopped on Sunday, and saw to my surprise, on a hill just opposite the enemy, that a deep, broad trench had been run within a few rods of them. In the sap were negroes digging it on still closer; and a company of infantry, returning, close at hand, the fire of the rebs. While I was taking

my observations, suddenly Bivins turned up at the foot
of the bank, cutting poles to pitch his shelter-tent with ;
and from him I learned that it was no other than our
old Company D that I could see loading and firing ;
pushed up, to say the least, among the very whiskers
about this old lion's active and well-armed jaws.

You shall go with me into this outmost sap, and
know what sights and sounds it is our business now to
be familiar with. Into this sap I am obliged to go three
times a day for my rations, out of the retreat of the
colors. First we must creep out of our ravine, through
the top of this prostrate tree, whose boughs catch our
clothing ; then up by the charred trunk, the feet slipping
in the mud. Your head now comes within the range
of riflemen in the trees over there. Sometimes they are
in the trees, though not always. A few steps more, and
we come within full range from the parapet ; but do not
stop to look. Stoop as low as you can, and run. This
stump will shelter you ; pitted with the striking of balls
against it, as if it had the small-pox when a sapling.
When you have caught your breath, run for that trunk.
It is an ugly one to get over ; for it is breast-high,
and one's whole body has to come into the enemy's view.
Once over this, and the road is smoother. We soon
gain the cover of the woods, and are comparatively safe.
The other day, I was twice shot at while passing the
space we have just been over. I do not know how near
the bullets came ; only the first seemed as if it were
sweeping my legs off at the knee with its sharp rush.
I stooped, and labored through the brush ; when the

second came cold along the length of my spine, just above the vertebræ. We are to have a better road, however. One of Company E has just been shot through the head — dead in an instant — here, and we are to have a protected passage-way.

Down this little gully, and we enter the beginning of the sap, at the end of the military road. Behind the angle, just back there, is the station of the ambulance-men. They wait there, day and night, with stretchers ready. These stretchers are now all blood-stained. Three or four a day, out of the brigade and working-party, are carried out. The ambulance-corps is made up largely of the musicians: but music! we never hear it now, not even the drum and fife. It is too stern a time for that.

We pass out into the sap. Here is the most danger-ous point of all, just at the entrance, where the first man from our regiment was killed the day of the assault. You see how the rebel parapet commands it. We are going considerably nearer to it; but we shall be better sheltered. 'Tis just in front, with an old shot-pierced building behind it, and white sand-bags lying on top of the tawny slope. That old building *might* be a ruinous mill, and those bags *might* be grist, laid out there along the wall until the miller was ready for it; but, every bag or two, there is a sharp-eyed Mississippian with his rifle pointed through some chink. Let us go at a good pace, so that no one of those fellows will have a chance to draw a bead on either of us. The trench goes under a large trunk, stretching from bank to bank; and from here we are tolerably safe. Only tolerably: for the other day, close by here, one of our company was hit in the face by a glancing ball; and Sergt. Bennett, of Company **K**, was mortally wounded by a fragment from one of our own shells, which flew back into our lines from over the rebel parapet, where the shell exploded. We are coming close, you see. Climb a steep pitch now, and we reach the station of Company **D.** The sap is here about six feet wide and four deep, dug out of the hard soil, the dirt being thrown out on the side *toward* the enemy; forming a bank rising about five feet from the surface, and therefore about nine feet above the bottom of the trench. Here now are our boys, the few that are left, — barely twenty. Along the top of the ridge of earth, logs are placed; into the under side of which, notches are cut at intervals of three or four feet; leaving, between the earth below and the timber above, a loop-hole, four or five inches in diameter, for the men to fire through. McGill has just sprung down, after discharging his piece. Before he loads again, let us climb up, and take a view of the world through the hole. Carefully ! Lay your body up against the steeply sloping bank, resting the feet on the edge of the sap. By all means, take care that the top of your head does not project above the narrow timber. Your face is at the hole now. From the outside, a groove runs along the top of the thick bank; then comes the open air; and opposite you, within call easily enough, is the deadly ridge; the two or three tents behind it; the old, ruinous chimneys, the one or two shattered buildings, — so near, you can plainly see threads and bricks and splinters. Do not look long. Every yard, perhaps the intervals are less, behind the sand-bags, there is a rifleman. Mellen, of Company F, has just been shot while aiming his piece through one of these holes. The ball entered through the hole, hit the band of his gun, then the lock, splintering wood and steel, then crashed in through his chest.

McGill is capping his gun. Try one more look before he jumps up for another shot. Can you see any one? No head, I'll warrant; for, though they are brave enough over there, they are not often careless. The most you will be likely to see will be a hand put up for a moment, with a ramrod, as the charge is pushed home; or a glimpse of butternut as a fellow jumps past some interval in the sand-bags. Now let McGill and Buffum and Wivers and the others, whose place it is, blaze away at whatever they can see. Little Gottlieb offers me his piece to try a few shots : but I am not anxious to kill a man; and, so long as it is not in my place to fire, I decline it.

You duck your head now as the balls whistle over. It is a nervous sound; but you would soon get over that here. They go with a hundred different sounds through the air, according to the shape, size, and velocity of the projectile. Two strike the bank. It is like two quick blows of a whip-lash. That went overhead, sharp as the cut of a cimeter; another goes with a long moan, then drops into the earth with a "thud." It comes from some more distant point, and is nearly spent. A

shot comes from some great gun in the rear, — an earthquake report; then the groaning, shuddering rush of
the shell, as if the air were sick and tired of them, and
it was too much to be borne that they should be so constantly sent.

Sit on the edge of the trench now, with your feet
hanging down, and your back leaning against the pile
of earth. The boys have built shelters of boughs, just
on the other side, to keep off, a little, the intolerable
sun. A line of men goes along the sap, each carrying
a fascine. Then comes a party rolling hogsheads filled
with cotton. These are built into the bank beyond to
give it strength. Steve and Tom, the cooks, come up
with dinner, which is cooked back in the woods to the
rear. Coffee and stewed beans to-day. There! — a
shower of dirt falls over us, dinner and all, from a ball
that hit near the loop-hole: but to dirt and balls alike
we are growing indifferent; so we only laugh.

But let us go out to the end of the sap. We pass
the young captain of engineers, who is in charge here;
a pleasant, active young fellow, who nods back to us as
we give him the salute, make several turns, and presently are at the end. Negroes are making the trench
here wider. We push through them to the cotton-
stuffed hogshead at the extremity. They roll this forward a foot or two, then dig out behind it, and so on.
A lieutenant of engineers, and a negro, have just been
shot here. From this crevice we can get a peep. Is
it not near? You can easily throw a hard-tack across.
Looking back on to a side-hill, we can see some of the

old wreck of the assault, — a rusty gun or two, mouldy equipments, and there a skeleton. Some regiments got very near on the 14th. Close by runs the little, disused path, among weeds and wild-flowers, along which, before we came, the garrison used to go from their works to the road. It looks innocent as the path up Pocumtuc; but what a way of death it would be to him who should get out of the sap, and try to walk in it! Our boys in the sap here have distinguished company. Almost every day, Gen. Banks comes through, — sometimes with quite a retinue, sometimes only with Gen. Stone.

"Well, boys, how do you stand it?" said he, the other day, to our men.

"Arrah, now, your honor," said Pat O'Toole, "we're most dead intirely for the want of whishkey."

We wait and watch. When night comes, I climb out of the ravine on to the hillside, where the air is fresh. There is a bright moon now, and my vigil is sure to be well lit. I am often there at midnight; and on the rebel side, faint and far along distant roads, I hear the low rattle of wheels, and call of drivers; and the sound of the active mill too, whose location the batteries are crazy to know, that they may seal its doom.

July 6. — The interest of campaigning I find to be of a spasmodic sort, — a few days of excitement and intense labor, then long periods of tedious inactivity. The interval since the skirmish near Jackson has been an uninteresting period, because its experiences are of a sort to which we have become accustomed, and of

which we have grown tired. Our life is a monotony
of perilous exposure. The regiment remains in its
advanced position, constantly under fire, and occasionally losing a member, killed or wounded. Meantime,
the engineers have been pushing forward their work.
What would have become of us, if the work of siege
had fallen to us to do, I do not know: or, rather, it is
easy to see what would have become of us, — hundreds
and hundreds in hospitals, or silent under brown
mounds; mounds which, as it is, have become numerous
on hillsides, and wherever the ground is open and at
all easy to the shovel.

Sambo, however, has saved us many lives. These
big black fellows, with arms like our legs almost, and
with muscle piled in great layers about rib and back,
have done the main work. The soil through which the
sap runs is very hard, — a tough, unyielding clay, upon
which a shovel makes but little impression.

Almost every crumble of it, it has been necessary to
hew out with a pickaxe. Sambo, however, is equal to
it. He has the courage to stand close to the rebel rifle-
pits all the time, and the strength to handle this unyielding earth.

Every morning and every night, the long fatigue-parties from the black engineer troops relieve each other;
and day by day, as we look out from our hiding-places,
we can see that the line of our sap runs farther and
farther. Two "cavaliers" have also been constructed.
These are elevations, built up of hogsheads, tier above
tier, designed to give sharpshooters a position from

which they can fire well within the parapet. The brunt of the work the negroes do. There are white overseers; and fatigue-parties, too, are detailed from white regiments: but, for the most part, we have had it for our work to keep sharp watch from our cover, and never allow a rebel head to appear above the opposite parapet, without a pointed leaden hint to withdraw, insinuated without ceremony through a loophole.

We keep hearing of the new assault. The army began to prepare for it at once, after the 14th of June. It was then supposed it would take place almost immediately; but it has been deferred. Tuesday evening, June 30, I had been for an hour or two at the camp, in the woods back from the front, where the convalescents of the regiments are quartered. Returning to my post about sunset, I found the road full of troops. A division had assembled to hear a speech from the commanding general. The gloss of military show had all worn off. The men were brown, — attired as they chose to be, — shaggy and stained with their bear-like life in ravines and behind logs. There were no flags or music, no shining brass or glossy broadcloth and lace. If glory lies in these things, "Ichabod" was written in deep, emphatic lines on the whole company.

But these were the stout Fourth Wisconsin, and Thirty-first Massachusetts, and other decimated regiments, that had faced rifle-muzzles in the two previous deadly assaults, and had all the heart in the world for another. If glory lies in that, every tanned and uncombed platoon abounded in it. Presently there was a stir, and the general rode up, iron as ever, in rough, serviceable dress; the gray moustache on his upper lip cropping out like a ledge of the metal, almost pure. He made a speech: —

"We were close on another assault. It was sure to be successful. if the army would do as well as it had done. Then would come rest, and the campaign would close in light."

Still we wait. A day or two after that, I walked down one branch of the sap to Duryea's battery of regulars, — seven twelve-pounders, — which had been dragged in through the narrow trench to an advanced point, where they threatened the rebels close at hand. As I went along, a rebel shell exploded in the air overhead, the pieces falling here and there into the bushes and into the dust. In the air where the shell burst, a halo of white, compact smoke floated for a minute or two, — a round, perfect ring, from which depended a fringe of less compact vapor, that floated longer and longer, and swayed to and fro, beautiful as a bridal veil hanging from a crown. The battery lay behind its embrasures. silent. Before each piece, the embrasure was hidden by a plate of iron, in which was a hole of the size of the muzzle of a gun, temporarily covered with a sand-bag. A rain of rifle-balls was being showered on the spot. I did not stay long; for that morning the battery-men told us they had lost three. They were waiting and waiting, with their cartridges at hand, and their fierce shells in piles, ready for their deadly flight.

Another day, I went through another branch of the sap to the mine. The passage was guarded against all but workmen ; but, fortunately, I met the colonel near the sentry, and he passed me in. I went through the zigzag passages, passed piles of fascines, and a pontoon bridge which lay ready to be put together across any ditch, when the day shall come for the charge.

At last I came to a turn, and found the parapet straight ahead. The sap ended in the mine, — a hole about four feet square, where a party of men were burrowing under the enemy's earthwork. I stooped, and looked in at the mouth. Negroes, on their knees, were working there by candle-light, excavating a place in which are to be put kegs of powder. With these it is designed to blow the parapet into the air, leaving a passage for our troops. It was a perilous place. The workmen all spoke in whispers, as they do in powder-mills. Sometimes the rebs toss over hand-grenades. Capt. Morton, with a squad, was at work there, placing sandbags. A short time after, in this very place, his lieutenant and some of his men were marked for life by the explosion of a hand-grenade.

Still the days pass, and no order is given. We imagined 4th of July would be the day; but it was not. Nor was it Sunday, the day following; nor Monday, to-day. The regiment is growing blue. This week, our time is out ; and the idea is spreading, that there is no going home for us till the place falls. There are some insubordinate threats ; but many of us feel as if our personal honor is concerned, and are determined not to go till the place falls, no matter when it happens. To-day, Port Hudson seems more impregnable than ever. The space within those stubborn banks, gullied by the rains and baked by the suns, so terribly edged with fire, as yet is unapproached and unapproachable.

To-night, Company D have all been in tears. Cyrus Stowell, the "pleasant corporal," so called for his unfailing amiability, on duty on our middle picket-post, thrown out upon the very mouths of the rebel rifles, suddenly, just at sundown, was shot through the head; his pure, sweet young life swept off in an instant. We dug his grave late this evening, by the light of tapers dimly burning, on the brow of a hill crowned by the old rifle-pits of the enemy, out of which we had forced them. Overhead was the clear light of stars.

On the horizon a tempest was gathering, — swelling accumulations of thunder-charged cloud lit up each moment from within with sudden luminousness, and rumbling with coming storm. Close at hand, through the agitated air, hurtled the constant roar of the siege. The body could not be brought out till after dark, as it was necessary to pass several exposed places.

It came at last, late at night, upon a stretcher borne by his comrades. We wrapped his young, tall figure in his tent, and laid him to rest. As we stood uncovered, during the service, close overhead swept the rifle-balls, until we thought there would be some new victim to be buried beside him.

CHAPTER XV.

TRIUMPH.

JULY 8. — The drama of Port Hudson I imagine to be pretty much played out. Yesterday our company had come out from the advance to rest. Suddenly an orderly passed through a group of us sitting near the colonel's quarters, hurrying with despatches to the different commanders of the brigade. McGill rushed out, and read the despatch as he carried it in his hand. It was, "Vicksburg surrendered on the Fourth!" Every pale, haggard face lit up with a wonderfully jolly light. Presently the brigadier hurried into the trenches; and a soldier, on duty at the mine, by his command, threw the news over among the rebels. At noon, we had a great firing of salutes. This morning, before light, we heard that a conference of the generals was to be held to agree upon the terms of surrender, and that a truce was to begin at once. The major went off through the dark to order the sharpshooters to stop firing; while we rubbed our eyes, wondering if the day had really come, — if our cause had really gained this great success, and we could go home with credit.

July 12. — In Port Hudson at last ! There was no false alarm. Vicksburg really fell on the 4th inst. On the 8th, down went Port Hudson ; and the particular work for which we came here was at last accomplished, just as our term of service expired. Glory be to God !

I write on the bold Port-Hudson bluff, within a step or two of the precipice, which descends seventy feet to the water's edge. My back is resting against the earthwork which protected one of the great cannon of the rebels. Before me rolls the great river ; the bluff here commanding a splendid reach of it, five or six miles up toward Vicksburg. From the water and the green woods that fringe it comes a cool breeze. Our work is done ; our time has expired ; and now we only wait for the sick of the regiment to be assembled, for the baggage to be collected, and for the arrival of the transports to take us North.

I am weary and worn with the siege and hard fare ; but the experiences of the last few days have been so interesting, that I must make some record of them.

As I have written, before daybreak, the morning of the 8th of July, the major went into the rifle-pits to stop hostilities, as the conference of the commanding generals was about to begin under a flag of truce. About sunrise, I hurried down the military road, and through the obstructed pathways, to the position of the regiment. The ravines were empty. I climbed up past the forsaken booths and caves to the outer picket-posts, and found the men were all out in front. There was

10

no need, this morning, of crouching. The rebel works were only a stone's-toss off; but the rebels themselves were walking and standing in the plainest sight, and free communication was going forward between the two armies.

A most complete *entente cordiale* had just been established between Company D and the Alabama and Arkansas men who have been posted opposite to us. It was rather embarrassing, at first, to come face to face with the chaps, who, for a month back, have been shooting at you night and day: but I wanted to study the live "reb," and determine the category in natural history under which he should come, — whether "gorilla," as some claim; or "chivalry," as others; or something between.

I passed out from behind an uprooted tree, the grass near the stump yet pressed down, where the body of Stowell fell as he was shot; then pushed on for a hollow, about half way to the rebel works, having an uncomfortable sense of insecurity as I walked upright, for it had become second nature to us to crawl and stoop. It was only a few steps. Here they were, the real truculent and unmitigated reb, in butternut of every shade, from the dingy green which clothes the unripe nut, to the tawny brown and faded tan which it wears at other stages, — butternut mixed with a dull characterless gray. There was no attempt at uniform, yet something common, in the dress of the whole company, — a faded look, as if the fabric, whatever its original hue, had felt the sun until all life and brightness had wilted in the web and been killed out of the dye. Still the clothing was whole; and, upon closer inspection, looked strong and serviceable, though very coarse.

A group of rebels were gathered in the hollow; and over the parapet others came jumping, coming in a straggling line down the slope. I am bound to say, they seemed like pleasant men. All were good-natured, and met our advances cordially. They straightened up as we did. "It was good to be able to stretch up once more to the full height: they had not been able to do it for a month." Several were free-masons; and there was mysterious clasping and mighty fraternizing with the brethren on our side. Some had been in Northern colleges, and were gentlemen; and even the "white trash" and "border ruffians," who made up the mass of them, were a less inhuman set than I should have believed.

The officers, sometimes, wore a uniform of gray; the rank being indicated by badges upon the collar. Sometimes there was nothing to distinguish them from privates. They were brown and dusty; though no more so than we, who, like them, had lived in burrows, on our backs and stomachs, for a month. We really thought, that in condition they went ahead of us. The climate and hard marching had sallowed and dug into our cheeks and shaken us on our pins; whereas they were, though not fat, by no means gaunt and emaciated. Still they hinted at rats, mule meat, and other hard matters, they had been forced of late to come down to.

"Here comes Old Thous'n Yards!" said they, as a

broad, tall Arkansian, with a beard heavy as Spanish moss on an oak, and a quick, dark eye, came swinging down from the parapet. They all made way for him with some deference. He was "Old Thous'n Yards" with every one, and turned out to be the great sharp-shooter of that part of the works. I inquired about him, and found he was a famous backwoodsman and hunter, who, with a proper rifle, was really sure of a bear or buffalo at the distance of a thousand yards. He came forward rather bashfully. On both sides, the rifles were left behind; and "Old Thousand Yards" seemed to be as much troubled to dispose of his hands as a college freshman at his first party. His left arm would half bend into a hollow as if to receive the rifle-barrel, and the right fingers work as if they wanted to feel the touch of the lock. I borrowed a chew of tobacco, and won the perennial friendship of "Old Thousand Yards" by bestowing it upon him. Then I bought his cedar canteen to preserve as a souvenir of Port Hudson and its sharpshooter. I fear more than one of our poor fellows has felt his skill; but, for all that, he was a good-natured fellow, with a fine frame and noble countenance, — a physique to whose vigor and mascu-line beauty, prairies and mountain-paths and wild chases had contributed.

For the most part, these men of the Forty-ninth Alabama and Fifteenth Arkansas seemed like honorable fellows, firm to their cause; disposed to be good-natured, but declining to give communications likely to help us; and, although owning to great hardship, apparently ready to fight on. They complimented our sharp-shooting. It killed and wounded far more than our shells had done; though our shells had burned stables here, a camp there, houses elsewhere, and dismounted many guns. They told us their rifles were Belgian, Enfield, and Springfield. They had no "target," or Kentucky rifles. as we had imagined. They evidently respected us, and we did them, — so brown and strong: some of them, indeed, with lack-lustre eyes, soap-locks, and lank frames, according to the conventional type of the Southerner; but plenty of them hearty, bright, and frank.

I came back at last to our covert, took a drink of rebel water out of "Old Thousand Yards'" canteen, and found my hostility to these fellows much mitigated. I could see why commanders generally frown on this sort of communication. It is likely to establish relations altogether too brotherly for the purposes of war. The great principle involved is liable to sink out of sight before the personal friendship.

Meantime, the generals conferred. At noon, a hitch was rumored, and we feared the re-opening of the tedious and terrible siege; but in the afternoon came better news, and at sundown the regiments began to gather from dens and caves, from thickets and ravines, — far and near, — and burnish up a little for a triumphal entry on the morrow.

The morrow came. We left the woods; the filthy little brook whose banks had been covered with the cooking booths of whole divisions of men, and which we had daily drunk almost dry; the graves and the rifle-pits, the half-completed saps, and dreary ovens in which the sun had baked us so long. We left them; henceforth, through long generations probably, to be objects of historical interest, mementoes of the great war. With the old flag, in Wilson's hands, spreading its soiled and tattered fragments to the breeze, a sick and diminished company, we marched through the gate, over tracks marked out by our shell, through riddled camps, past carcasses of horses, and new-made graves of men; then drew up in line, at last, on the brink of the bluff, with the great, liberated river rolling before us toward the sea.

> " We were but warriors for the working-day:
> Our gayness and our gilt were all besmirched
> With rainy marching in the painful field.
> There was no piece of feather in our host,
> And time had worn us into slovenry;
> But, by the Mass! our hearts were in the trim."

July 13. — Since the army entered Port Hudson, I have taken two long rambles: the first, to the corner of the works opposite our " right centre," the point at which we were stationed; the other, to what is called the " citadel," at the southern end of the defences on the river-bank. It was only very strong curiosity that drew me out for these walks. We all find ourselves much debilitated. Our fare, always hard enough, has lately been harder than ever. About the time of the surrender, there was a period of some days during which I tasted nothing but our hard-bread — which now is often wormy — and our coarse coffee. Fat salt-pork, indeed, was served out to us; but that, for me, is out of the question, in this climate. We are just finding out, now, the strait we were in. The rebels had actually blocked up the river at Donaldsonville, and destroyed our communications with New Orleans, whence we draw all our supplies, when Port Hudson surrendered.

The day after our entrance, however, I forgot my weakness, so far as I could, and started with Grider and McGill out upon the line of the Clinton and Port-Hudson Railroad for the "works." I ought to say, that we find Port Hudson to be a little cluster of perhaps forty or fifty houses, on the edge of the bluff. The line of rebel intrenchments extends about this in the form of an irregular semicircle, — beginning on the river-bank, then running well back into the country, and returning to strike the bluff two or three miles below the village. The length of the line of intrenchments is said to be about seven miles. As we left the neighborhood of the little village, the country grew wild, cut and crossed, like the ground we had occupied outside, with ravines and little watercourses. The carcasses of animals were abundant, making the air foul; and often we came to old camps, — rows of huts built of logs and mud. Many of the huts were pierced by our shot, which seem to have penetrated to every part of the space within the enclosure. Every few steps, the foot trod upon a fragment of exploded shell, or a Parrott bolt, or round shot. Not far from the breastwork, we came to a redoubt which contained a ruined cannon.

It was a large siege-piece, facing, through its embrasure, one of our cavaliers, which contained, I remember, a formidable Parrott gun. This poor cannon was deeply dented here and there throughout its length, its carriage splintered; and it was turned on to its side, so that the trunnions were vertical. The last shot of our Parrott, so the rebels told us, had struck at the muzzle, just splintering the lip of the piece, then fairly entering the bore. We could feel an obstruction in the bore of the gun, with the rammer, which we supposed was the bolt. We were told that the shot struck just as a brave and skilful officer was sighting the piece; and that a certain dark stain, still visible on the earth near by, was his life-blood, poured out then and there. This cannon was not upon the outer intrenchments. The precision of our artillery-fire, the rebels assure us, was something wonderful; and we found ample evidence of it. Every gun at all exposed was sure to be detected by the sharp eyes of our cannoneers; and then its fate was sealed. At last, the rebels only dared to place their guns in the rear, concealing their whereabouts as much as possible: but then they were not safe, as in the case of this piece.

From this point, we soon came to the memorable angle where our sap approached. Every step, the evidences of the past storm became more numerous. The trees had lost their tops, the shells had hollowed out huge holes in the ground, and even weeds and bushes showed where the fire had swept. We came fairly to the outer works: and here the appearance of things was

as if a tornado had swept across, whose hail had had
the power to penetrate every thing; or rather as if
the spot had received such a fiery storm as fell upon
Sodom and Gomorrah. The few trees still standing
were splintered into match-wood up their sides, or had
lost their tops; and, in some cases, the solid balls had
pierced them through and through, leaving them standing, tall and thick, with perforated trunks! The rough
buildings near, which we had been able to see so plainly,
were shattered in every way; and hardly a square foot
could be found upon their timbers not marked by a bullet.
The surface of the earth was ploughed and seared;
the sand-bags on the breastwork, that I have looked
at so often from our cover, were pierced and powder-
stained; and, in the old rifle-pits, bloody sacking told
where there had been killed and wounded men. It
was very interesting to look over toward our approaches
and hiding-places. Here ran our sap, touching at last
the parapet; there rose the outside of the towering cavalier; there was the pile of cotton-bales, protecting an
exposed part of the military road, behind which I had
often crept; and there (how very close and plain!) was
the prostrate tree where Cyrus Stowell was shot. I
must have stood in the very tracks of the riflemen who
did it. It was a little melancholy to think of the haunts
as abandoned that had held so much life; where, for
twenty-five days, we had undergone peril and hardship.
We found the rebels had had no better cover than we,
and that our fire had been more sharp and deadly even
than theirs.

The preparations the rebels had been making against our third assault were in plain view here. We knew they had been hard at work. Mysterious sounds had come over into our sap; and a pickaxe or shovel would occasionally be thrust up into view, over the parapet. Where the breach was to have been made, a space of ground was thickly planted with hard-wood stakes, sharply pointed. A second parapet, for riflemen, had been constructed, and a cannon posted to throw grape. In the ground were buried enormous shell, ready to be discharged. The wires connecting with these ran near our feet, and we were forced to step with care. Had Heaven been a little less kind, it would have been our fate to charge at this very spot.

The "Citadel," at the southern end of the intrench-ments, was the goal of an excursion on the day following. It was a walk of a mile and a half. Here the siege operations had been of greater magni-tude than at our approach. The effects of the enor-mous artillery of the fleet appeared as they could not be seen elsewhere. Here, too, the rebels had placed along the bluff their most formidable guns, — the mouths that had spoken so thunderously the doom of the "Mis-sissippi," stranded on the shore opposite there, that night in March, when we listened in the woods. We found great cavities, where the large bombs had ex-ploded. If the earth was soft, it is not exaggerating much to say that these were large enough for cellars to small houses. If the earth was hard, they were large enough to make rifle-pits for a soldier. We came to smooth, round holes, a foot or so in diameter, bored down into the earth out of sight. I thought, at first, they were ventilators to some deep bomb-proof or sub-terranean passage of the enemy; but they were too numerous and too irregularly disposed for that. They were made by descending shot. Presently we found some projectiles, — gigantic bolts of iron, — two feet long and eight inches thick, and cone-shaped at one end. We could not begin to lift them, nor many of the fragments of the exploded shells.

The shells were the missiles whose wonderful flight I had watched so often, alone, at midnight, from the top of the slope above the ravine of the color-guard. The southern horizon would light up with the wide-spreading glare of the discharge; then came the majestic plane-tary sweep of the ascending bomb, revealed by its revolving fuse, far into the zenith, — the deep, swinging roar, the stern music of the rushing sphere; then the awful fall from the perihelion of its tremendous orbit, and the earthquake crash at last! In such manner, once perhaps, a circling world, with fire-charged heart, burst into the asteroids!

As we approached the southern defences, we found them to be evidently of older construction and more formidable character than the defences we had before seen. The citadel was an outlying work, in front of a double or triple line of parapets. Less than an eighth of a mile opposite, across a depression, was a seventeen-gun battery of ours, which had added its force to that of the fleet. From this battery, toward the river, ran a trench, perhaps forty rods in length. Opening from the trench, a zigzag sap approached the citadel, — so dug that troops could come up to its walls without exposure. The approach touched the hostile parapet, and ended in a mine, which was nearly completed at the time of the surrender; and ran — a deep resounding cavern — far under the feet of the defenders. It was designed, by means of this, to blow this whole part of the fortification into the air.

The clash of the hostile forces here had been tremendous. It was impossible to think of the Northern power, except as a terrible fiery tide, which, responding to some tempest-breathing of God, had hurled itself upon this outpost. I came when the storm was gone, and could see the mark of the sublime impact. The sea had torn its ragged, zigzag way through the bosom of hill and plain, — dashed against battlement and cliff, and roared at the base, until it had hollowed out for itself deep-penetrating channels. Everywhere it had scattered its fiery spume. Within the citadel lay siege-guns and field-pieces, broken and dented by blows mightier than those of trip-hammers; wheels, torn to bits; solid oaken beams, riven as by lightning; stubborn parapets, dashed through almost as a locomotive's plough dashes through a snow-drift, — these, and the bloody garments of men.

A photographist was quietly taking pictures on the parapet; one or two soldiers were strolling about: but the storm was gone, — the sapper gone from the mine, the gunner from beside his cannon-wheel, the rifleman from his sand-bag, still smutched from the muzzle of his piece. Then, as we came back, we saw the fierce, gray-headed old colonel, now our prisoner, who had commanded here, and breasted all this infernal force.

CHAPTER XVI.

CONCLUSION.

OUR work was done. The regiment languished for two or three weeks, — first upon the bluff; then upon a hot, pestilential plain, far back within the fortress. Day by day, men fell sick of fever, or worn out for the want of proper food. Day by day, we laid away the dead; and it was plain more must die, unless we could soon go northward.

At length, the forenoon of the 23d of July, while we were burying poor Spencer Phelps, dead of terrible fever just at the moment when relief was at hand, the transport touched at the Levee, which was to take us North. At dusk, we left the tents and the graves, the long parapet with our rifle-pits beyond, and the barren, sun-baked bluff. We marched aboard, a nerveless, debilitated company, too weak and sick to show joy even at going home.

Grosvenor, indeed, my good friend, a high-minded patriot, whose great spirit had carried his feeble body through all our exposures, though pale and haggard, went from man to man, shaking hands. He lay down at night, spreading out his blankets with his old comrades. In the morning, his couch lay as he had spread it; but he was gone, and the eyes of no man have rested upon him since. His was a brave and knightly soul. No doubt he rose in the night, too exultant, perhaps, over the brighter prospects of our great cause, and over the thought that hardship honorably borne was soon to be over, to sleep. The moon, about full, floated gloriously before him in the heavens, among the summer clouds, as the "Sangreal, with its veils of white samite," floated before Arthur's pure-souled knights. A misstep with his weak limbs, and he fell overboard into the flood. So our good friend must have perished.

Steadily we pushed northward. A large space, where it was most airy, was given up for a hospital, and crowded with the sick. Here was my post at night, from seven to one. One night, three worn-out soldiers gave up the ghost; but the wind, as we drew forward, blew more cool, and the air of home began to have its effect.

We looked off upon Natchez and battered Vicksburg; upon gunboats patrolling, and at anchor off dangerous shores. Then came Memphis; and in a day or two, a week after we had begun our voyage up those long leagues, we reached Island Ten and Columbus, — the hostile strongholds of two years before.

We left nearly a score of our more deathly sick to the Sisters of Charity at Mound City; then on through "Egypt," where they did not care for us; across through loyal Indiana and Ohio, where they cheered and clasped us, and only blamed us because we had sent no word of our coming. Flourish, little Marion! where every villager came running to us, who were so worn and hungry, with a well-filled basket; and blessings on generous Buffalo! city of prodigious gains and prodigious munificence, where, on Sunday morning, a congregation and their shepherd held service at the depot, ministering with tearful eyes to the sallow and fever-smitten multitude.

And now we are nearing home. Hark! it is my own church-bell, ringing welcome. Here are the familiar faces at last. Old Cruden and venerable Calmet welcome their master from their shelves; and ere long, washed and refreshed, the soldier falls on his knees, by the side of his own sweet, white bed, to thank God for his mercies.

The Banks campaign of the spring and early summer of 1863 is coming to be looked upon as a masterpiece of strategy. As yet, but little has appeared in print about it. It ought, however, to interest the military student and the general public. Facts, I think, will support the interpretation of the campaign, which I propose to give. If the view about to be presented is correct, to Gen. Banks, in addition to his former fame, is due the glory of being a mighty leader of armies.

Gen. Banks was sent to Louisiana to hold and govern the territory which had already been conquered by Butler and Farragut, and to restore the Federal authority in regions still under the rebel domination. In the

way of offensive operations, the special task given him
to perform was to co-operate with Grant in re-opening
the Mississippi. Vicksburg and Port Hudson were the
two obstacles to be overcome. To Grant was intrusted
the reduction of the former; to Banks, the capture of
Port Hudson.

During the inclement weather of the winter, the army
was arriving. The regiments, as they came, went into
camp, and were vigorously drilled. In March, when
the heavy rains had ceased and military operations became possible, Banks was ready to take the field. His
force consisted only of the Nineteenth Army Corps. A
good part of this force were "nine-months' men," whose
terms of service expired during the first part of the
summer. Whatever was done, must be done before
midsummer.

At this time, Gardner held Port Hudson with a force
equal to, or perhaps greater than, the army which Gen.
Banks could bring against him. To rush at once upon
the enemy, within his strong intrenchments, would have
been to incur certain and bloody defeat. It was an
occasion for strategy. *Port Hudson could be reduced,
if Gardner could be led to send away a considerable part
of his garrison; and if, at the same time, it could be so
managed, that the remnant left should be short for supplies,
so that protracted resistance would be impossible.* How to
accomplish this was the problem before the general,
in the beginning of March, when he prepared for active
operations.

The first operation of the campaign was directed

toward cutting off the river communication of the garrison, by which they could receive supplies and re-enforcements.   The 13th of March, we set out from Baton Rouge for Port Hudson.   At dusk of the 14th, the reader of the foregoing pages will remember, we were pushed up to within easy cannon-range of the rebel batteries ; while field-artillery fired and manœuvred as if a rush were to be made at once upon the parapet. *We* expected a land-attack ; the enemy expected it.   A bright reb, whom I met, during the truce on the morning of the capitulation, between their rampart and our rifle-pits, told me, that, so confident were they that night of a land-attack, the "cannoneers on the bluff were off their guard.   They did not see the fleet stealing silently past, until the vessels at the head were pretty much out of danger, up the stream.   If they had seen them, they could have kept them down as they did the ships farther back."   The next day, as I stood on the bold Port-Hudson bluff, and saw the immense guns which the rebels had planted on the brow, with delicate sights just above the enormous muzzles, and well-stored magazines, and ovens for hot shot close at hand, I could not help believing what the rebel had told me.   With those cannon, hot shot and shell could be cast, almost with the precision of rifle-balls, at objects passing below. If the cannoneers had kept sharp watch, the "Hartford" and "Albatross," both wooden vessels, could not have passed.   It was precisely that thing the general was manœuvring after, — to induce the garrison to look for a land-attack ; whereas the object he had in view was to get these powerful vessels above the fortress to cut off the river communication. It was the artifice, precisely, of a skilful boxer, who makes a feint with his right hand, then puts in the blow in earnest with his left. The stratagem was successful. The general, no doubt, wished to pass a stronger force of vessels above the fortress; but the two proved sufficient. The rebels had nothing on the stream to cope with them in fair fight, and Farragut was too sagacious and prudent to be entrapped. The "Mississippi," indeed, was lost; but one old frigate was a small price to pay for so substantial an advantage.

The next operation of the campaign was to manœuvre in such a way as to induce the rebel commanders to believe, that Port Hudson, after all, was not the threatened point. Now that the river was in our possession, the great garrison at Port Hudson would soon be embarrassed for supplies; and, if Gardner and Pemberton could be induced to believe that Banks had some project elsewhere, it would be the natural thing for them to withdraw a portion of the force from the distressed stronghold, and send them, by land, where they fancied the troops could be of more service.

Banks proceeded without delay. At the end of March, we embarked on transports, and went southward from the rebels, toward New Orleans. Landing at the Bayou La Fourche, we marched westward, and, in a week or two, began the raid through the back country, from Brashear City to Alexandria on the Red River. The inferior rebel force in this region was dissipated by our hasty rush ; a vast amount of cotton and sugar were captured ; and supplies were seized, which might possibly have found their way into Port Hudson, escaping the vigilance of the "Hartford" and "Albatross." But the most important end accomplished was this,—and it was, no doubt, the end which the general had mainly in view, — it completely misled the rebel generals as to his real designs.

The young rebel colonel, chief of Gardner's staff at Port Hudson, the night after the capitulation in July, rides over to the Federal camp to see his old friend and former companion-in-arms, Col. G——, of the ——th Mass. An old friend of mine, a distinguished young officer of the regiment, is present at the interview, and sits up himself with the rebel colonel, till midnight, talking over past events. Next time I see my friend, he tells me about his talk. One thing is this : This officer says, that, when Banks was at Alexandria, it was believed, on the rebel side, that Port Hudson was no longer threatened ; that, at that time, Lieut-Gen. Pemberton sent word from Vicksburg, to his subordinate, Gardner, that Port Hudson was not in danger, and that he might send elsewhere part of his army. Gardner did so ; and, when he was weakened by sending off a large portion of his force, suddenly Banks, on the Red River, put his army upon transports, and Port Hudson was invested, before a man of those who had been sent away could be recalled.

"Oh," said the rebs to us when the fortress fell, "if you had only attacked us when you came up in March, when we were ready for you!" But that was precisely what Gen. Banks was too wise to do. Instead of that, he had preferred to manœuvre so as to induce the rebel leaders to reduce the garrison, and to cut off their supplies of provisions

The field of all this manœuvring was very extensive. The Fifty-second Regiment marched more than three hundred miles while it was being done, and a portion of the army accomplished still more. Well do we remember what ache and sweat it cost us! But it was vigorous to the extent of human endurance, and perfectly successful; for at the end of May, when the sudden investment of Port Hudson took place, the place contained but a few thousand troops, with provisions for only a few weeks.

The third and closing operation of the campaign was the siege of Port Hudson. During this siege, two assaults were made upon the rebel works, — on the 27th of May and the 14th of June. Both were bloody; both were unsuccessful as assaults: and Gen. Banks has been blamed sometimes for having "mismanaged" them, sometimes for having suffered them to be made at all.

As to the charge of mismanagement. It should be remembered, that no military undertaking is more critical than an assault upon a well-defended fortress. In 1811, Wellington was twice repulsed at Badajoz, with prodigious loss; and in 1799, at Acre, Napoleon himself rushed seven or eight times in vain against the works defended by the British and Turks. Certainly it would be rash to say, simply because an assault was unsuccessful, that it was mismanaged. The opinion of competent military critics is alone of value upon this point. The writer is far enough from pretending to such a character. We used to hear, at Port Hudson, that the assaults failed from lukewarmness on the part of subordinates; from the irremediable embarrassment arising from the early and unexpected fall of officers holding important commands; and from the circumstance, that portions of the attacking force lost their way. To say the least, it is as probable that some such cause as this prevented success, as that there was want of skill in planning the attacks.

Gen. Banks has been blamed for having suffered the assaults to be made at all. Since an assault is so critical an affair, perhaps nothing is sufficient to justify one, but some great strait in which a general is placed. A siege is far safer and more certain, and ought, no doubt, to be preferred, when there is time. Was Gen. Banks in such a strait as to justify him in trying to storm Port Hudson? It is hard to see how a general can be in a much closer corner than was Gen. Banks at the end of May. At the outset of the campaign, his force was small, in view of the objects to be accomplished. The vigorous operations which took place at once had diminished this force very largely. The hot season had already begun; during which, sickness was sure to prevail. Moreover, the time of the "nine-months' men" was on the point of expiring. Is it strange Gen. Banks felt driven to even desperate expedients?

The assaults failed in their main object of taking the fortress, but still secured us some advantages. Each time, numbers of rebels fell, and important ground was gained close under the hostile parapet.

The siege was pushed as operations had been pushed from the beginning. Farragut kept watch above and below on the river, and no food could reach the half-starved garrison. From land and stream poured in a constant fire of shot and shell, while sharpshooters sent their volleys day and night. At length, the place fell. It was high time : for the nine-months' regiments were beginning to mutiny ; New Orleans, which was held by a small force, was seriously threatened ; and the whole army, under the burning heats, was fast sinking away. Out of our company of ninety, scarcely twenty were on duty at last. The whole regiment was diminished in the same proportion, and the men counted as effective were generally far below the standard of health ; yet there were few stronger regiments than ours. That the fall of Vicksburg, which took place a few days previous, only hastened the fall of Port Hudson by a day or two, we have the testimony of the rebel leaders, and the explicit declaration of Gen. Grant himself. The Nineteenth Army Corps claim for their general the full glory of the capture, — a success accomplished with a small comparative force, within a comparatively short time, under unfavorable skies. We claim for our leader the superlative merits of almost unexampled vigor, sagacity, courage, and persistence.

The day after the surrender, I saw the general ride

on his black steed, down the bluff, on his way to the
"Hartford," to exchange congratulations with his brave
and skilful coadjutor, the admiral.   He was haggard
and pale, as were his men; but strong and exultant.
So he rode, — the foremost man of New England;
perhaps the foremost man of the land: and so, I can
believe, rode Marlborough, after Blenheim; and Prince
Eugene at Belgrade.

During the past year, I have seen much of human
nature, — often a very rough side of it.   In our own
regiment were a large number of men of such age and
character as are not usually found in the position of
private soldiers; but we had, besides these, a proportion of "rough characters."   Then, again, in organi-
zations less favored than ours, with which we were
associated, there was ample opportunity of meeting with
those whom society calls very much debased.   I met
such men under circumstances when many of the ordinary restraints of life were taken off, so that their true
natures could come out more fully.   What have I
learned?   To put as much confidence in men as ever;
to believe in the intrinsic goodness of the human heart.
Indolence, cruelty, sensuality, meanness, are the things
men invariably detest, and what they blame.   Mercy,
liberality, truth, kindness, are what they invariably
commend.

Much evil there is among the rank and file, as there
is among those higher in position.   I have seen want
of patience, want of honesty, want of temperance.   I

have seen gambling and ill-temper, and know how foul the air of a camp is with coarseness and blasphemy. But this I have not seen : the man who liked or would commend selfishness ; the man who disliked or would blame unselfishness. One does not learn to think less of human nature from contact with "rough men," however it may be from contact with those at the opposite social extreme. Often they do not imitate what they admire ; often they do not avoid in their own conduct what they detest in others : but this is true, that the human instincts are always fixed in a love for good, in a hatred for bad. In the society of the low, as in every human society, there is but one rule for securing enduring popularity, — "Be unselfish."

I have known men, rough in language and manners ; judged by our conventional standards, thoroughly unsanctified ; perhaps they hardly ever saw the inside of a church, or breathed an audible prayer, though their talk was full of oaths : yet they would do noble things. They would help others generously ; they would bear privation cheerfully ; and I have known them, in a time of pestilence, to watch, day and night, with patients sick of contagious diseases, when the camp was full of death. They watched until they grew sick ; then, after they were sick, until their lives were in peril. I have heard the lips of dying men bless them.

The thought of the beautiful poem of "Abou Ben Adhem" is, that, because he loves his fellow-men, an angel writes his name at the head of the list of those whom "love of God had blessed." I know not why

11

the names of some of these I speak of should not be
written there too, "rough" though they are.

Now that all is over, let me set down, briefly, the
light in which the great question lies before me after
this experience. I find my face set persistently as ever
against the threatening power. Near observation only
confirms what we hear of its strength, of its iniquity,
of its persistent hostility to what we hold sacred. Of
the benefits I have derived from this military experience,
it is not the least, that now I know, through my own
observation, what before was only hearsay. We have
heard that Southern society was ignorant; that, at the
South, there was little regard for justice; that the heart
of the slaveholder became cruel and hard; that the
marriage-tie was held in small respect. We have
heard, too, about the effect of slavery upon the negroes;
that although it raised them, in a degree, above barbarism, — far enough to make them useful instruments,
forcing them into industry and into so much of order
and decency as improved them as tools, — yet that there
it left them, and interposed iron barriers against their
mounting farther in the scale. We have heard, that,
under slavery, there can be but one form of industry, —
the simplest agriculture; that here the tools are coarse,
the methods rude, the operations so carried on as soon
to impoverish the earth; that when the surface richness
is taken off, instead of replenishing its strength or sub-
soiling, the soil is simply abandoned, to become a
wilderness again, while the planter goes off in search
of virgin, inexhausted land.

All these things have been matters of hearsay; but now I can pile fact upon fact, from my own observation. in confirmation. If slavery is to exist, it must extend its area. There are inherent necessities which force it to seek new and again new domain. How lucidly and convincingly is this argued in "The Slave Power"! We must triumph, or, I believe in my heart, we shall see the triumphant South extending its dominion southward and westward into Mexico; thence, in the future, forced by these inherent necessities, into the other continent and the tropical islands, — extending its empire throughout the "golden circle" that surrounds the Gulf of Mexico. This territory, slavery will blast as it has blasted the territory in its possession to-day It will debase the master-class into the cruelty, the injustice, the corruptness, which we know now as characterizing them. It will maintain the servile class in a situation but little removed from their first barbarism.

I know not how, to-day, any knightly and chivalrous soul can do otherwise than burn to rush forth to prevent this. As I write, the cause of the slave-power languishes. It was otherwise up to the first days of July; or, rather, its decline was less marked than our safety required. I remember well, how in the rifle-pits, toward the end of June, I heard Grosvenor talk, who is now no more. Justice and truth, he held, were in peril as much as when we came forth; and could we go home, and leave it so? Rather ought we to stay, though amid hunger and fever and leaden rain, until light

came.   Almost in that very hour came the dawning
of light.   But if skies again darken, if through unfore-
seen disaster or alien interference the good cause is again
imperilled, ought we not to thank God we have learned
to endure the march, to poise the rifle, to bear up
against the hot, shrill hail of war?   So to live, in these
times, we feel is to live well ; and to die at the front is
to die well ; and, unto those who die thus, the voice of
Christ might say, —

> " Come, my beloved! e'en as I was pained,
>   So art thou broken, and thy life outpoured :
>   Therefore I bless thee, and give thanks for thee."

THE   END.

Boston: Printed by John Wilson and Son.

www.ingramcontent.com/pod-product-compliance
Lightning Source LLC
Chambersburg PA
CBHW030811020726
47499CB00006B/1872